The Tall Man in the Dark Suit

The World War II Ship Diary and Letters of a German Kriegsmarine Cadet

by Frauke Elber

To Jim and Nancy
in memory of all who did not come back
Frauke

TABLE OF CONTENTS

The Tall Man in the Dark Suit..1
   The World War II Ship Diary and Letters........................1
   of a German Kriegsmarine Cadet................................1
TABLE OF CONTENTS 2
INDEX OF PICTURES...3
INTRODUCTION 5
   The NEPA years 1932-1940......................................9
THE LOG BOOK...14
   SPERRBRECHER 1...15
   14 days of machine duty 42
LETTERS 84
THE SHIPS..88
   SPERRBRECHER 1...88
   Battleship GNEISENAU 90
   U-593 91
   U-436 93
   British Naval Archive records 95
Afterword..98
Acknowledgement 105
About the Author 106

INDEX OF PICTURES

Figure 1 Günter Braun age 9 months with mother (left) and aunt Martha ...7

Figure 2 Günter age 10 with sister Inge and their mother 8

Figure 3 Günter during his time at NPEA Oranienstein and father (about 1935) 8

Figure 4 Braun family about 1938..........................8

Figure 5 Castle Oranienstein which housed the NEPA 9

Figure 6 The dormitory building 9

Figure 7 The school's rowing team 10

Figure 8 Günter Braun and his younger charges 10

Figure 9 Morning roll call..........................11

Figure 10 Teacher's dining hall inside the castle 11

Figure 11 Gliding..........................12

Figure 12 Castle Chapel now..........................12

Figure 13 Student's dining hall inside the castle 12

Figure 14 Student's sleeping hall 13

Figure 15 Sperrbrecher 1 14

Figure 16 My maneuver station..........................16

Figure 17 Harbor entrance of Lorient 17

Figure 18 We escorted a U-boat out. Now it goes on its own power 18

Figure 19 Our flag on the mast..........................18

Figure 20 11 marks were on the bridge when we came on board. Now there are 14. Each mark means one mine. 19

Figure 21 Our 3.7 cm gun..........................20

Figure 22 Boom, our 5th mine explodes. 22

Figure 23 The M.P. at backboard 23

Figure 24 Airplane 180 degree, Aim 25

Figure 25 Stop Battery..........................25

Figure 26 The spill and the anchor chains..........................26

Figure 27 A U-boat comes back 27

Figure 28 "Mine" our board dog..........................27

Figure 29 The Captain on the bridge 30

Figure 30 1st Division lined up at the Wicklung for muster 31

Figure 31 Muster by the captain 32

Figure 32 The long swells of the Atlantic 33

Figure 33 The 2cm ready for firing 34

Figure 34 The distances are transmitted from the E-instrument to the batteries 35

Figure 35 cleaning gun 35
Figure 36 Fort Louis 36
Figure 37 The bow of our ship 36
Figure 38 2 tugboats guide us to the anchoring buoy 38
Figure 39 A minesweeper is leaving 38
Figure 40 On search cruise 39
Figure 41 We are meeting a scout boat 40
Figure 42 We detonated our 20th mine 41
Figure 43 The heaving line flies to land 42
Figure 44 Eiffel Tower 54
Figure 45 Grave of the unknown soldier 55
Figure 46 Arc de Triomphe 56
Figure 47 Tomb of Napoleon I and Dome des Invalides............................57
Figure 48 Tomb of Marshall Foch...57
Figure 49 Sacre Coeur and Basilica Notre Dame Cathedral 58
Figure 50 Our battlegroup on war march 67
Figure 51 Steaming through the Channel 68
Figure 52 GNEISENAU 69
Figure 53 Günter Braun: third front row, center...76
Figure 54 The author and her father 79
Figure 55 The author and her uncle Günter Braun Christmas 1942..........80
Figure 56 "The tall man in the dark suit" Günter Braun and his niece
    Frauke 81
Figure 57 Günter Braun and his friend Helga. The back of the picture is
    inscribed with: "to Frauke so she knows what her uncle Günter looks
    like." January 1943 81
Figure 58 Sperrbrecher 1 89
Figure 59 Gneisenau 91
Figure 60 Gerd Kelbig official portrait and after a war patrol 92
Figure 61 U-593 sinking...93
Figure 62 Günther Seibicke Official portrait and after a war patrol..........94
Figure 63 U-436 sinking...94
Figure 64 HMS TEST convoy KX 10 97
Figure 65 Günter Braun, March 1941...104
Figure 66 German U-boat Memorial Möltenort/ Germany 106
Figure 67 German U-boat Memorial Möltenort/ Germany Photos Heinz
    Potrafki...107

INTRODUCTION

Günter Braun, my uncle, was born on October 2, 1920. After World War I had ended, life in the big cities of Germany was full of turmoil, protests, shootings and lawlessness. Ongoing street battles made life as dangerous as the war itself. My grandfather sent his young pregnant wife and two- year- old daughter, my mother, to relatives in southern Germany where they found peace and safety on the big farm where my grandfather grew up. It was there that my uncle was born. I don't know much about his youth, except that he was not a scholarly young man. Therefore, when he reached high school age, my grandfather enrolled him in one of the party-run military academies, called NPEA (National Political Education Academy). From letters and photo albums that survived World War II, it seemed that these were great and challenging years for his young adventurous mind. He did not realize that these schools pursued the goal of producing upcoming leaders in the military and SS. What these schools offered the young people can never be duplicated today. They were boarding schools with strict discipline. The upperclassmen were responsible for their younger brethren. Sports were high on the list of the curriculum as were leadership and pre-military classes. Beside the traditional academic classes, the school offered horseback riding, boating and soaring. They also offered exchanges with students from foreign countries, countries that fit the Nazi ideology. What impressionable, adventurous youngster wouldn't have loved this? Günter graduated from this school and entered the German Navy (Kriegsmarine) as an officer cadet in summer of 1940.

He was over six feet tall, blond, handsome, the perfect image of Hitler's warped Aryan race ideal. He spent basic training at a naval school in the Baltic Sea port city of Stralsund and some of this time there on the tall mast ship GORCH FOCK. His first shipboard assignment was on SPERRBRECHER 1, a converted freighter used to clear mines from the shipping channels and serving as a floating class room for young naval cadets. The ship was based in Lorient,

France. It is on this ship on December 31, 1940 that his diary entries begin, giving a glimpse into the daily routine and practical training of naval cadets on a warship. Keeping a diary was required during the training.

His on-board training alternated with various courses at the Mürwick Naval Academy and several other naval schools.
His next shipboard assignment was on the pocket battleship GNEISENAU, home ported in the French harbor of Brest. The logbook gives an eyewitness account of the now famous Channel Dash of the three battleships SCHARNHORST, GNEISENAU and PRINZ EUGEN, and the bombing of the GNEISENAU in Kiel harbor. Because of the crew size on these ships (1600 men); he did not like the impersonal atmosphere and therefore volunteered for the U-boat force.

His wish was granted and he was assigned to U-593 in Saint Nazaire, France where his first war cruise almost became his last. Fate caught up with him when he was assigned to U-436 which was sunk in the North Atlantic on May 26, 1943, two days after all U-boats in the Atlantic were called back to their bases. He was 22 ½ years old.

His logbook entries end with his boarding U-593. After the loss of U-436 all his possessions that were left ashore, including the logbook, were sent to his parents, my grandparents. My grandfather continued the entries into the logbook on hand of letters and personal conversations with his son up to the demise of U-436.

After my grandparents' death the logbook was passed to my mother, Günter's older sister, and after her death in 1999 to me.

Now, 70 years later, this ship diary has become a historic document. I decided to donate it to the Mariners' Museum Library in Newport News, Virginia. For this purpose I translated the log book into English and while doing so found out more and more about the uncle I never knew and the time he lived in.

The following pages contain the logbook, letters, photos and archival documentation.

Frauke Elber
January 2013

Figure 1 Günter Braun age 9 months with mother (left) and aunt Martha

Figure 2 Günter age 10 with sister
Inge and their mother

Figure 3 Günter during his time at
NPEA Oranienstein and father
(about 1935)

Figure 4 Braun family about 1938

The NEPA years 1932-1940

Figure 5 Castle Oranienstein which housed the NEPA

Figure 6 The dormitory building

Figure 7 The school's rowing team

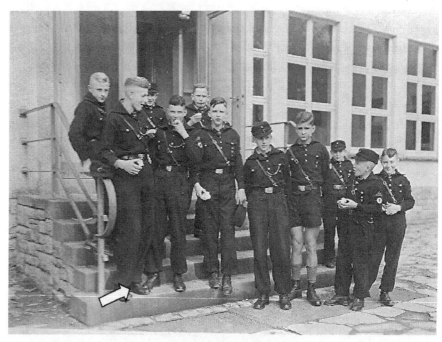

Figure 8 Gűnter Braun and his younger charges

Figure 9 Morning roll call

Figure 10 Teacher's dining hall inside the castle

Figure 11 Gliding   **Figure 12 Castle Chapel now**

Figure 13 Student's dining hall inside the castle

Figure 14 Student's sleeping hall

THE LOG BOOK

Figure 15 Sperrbrecher 1

SPERRBRECHER 1

New Year's Eve shortly before midnight.

I'm sitting comfortably with my comrades in the living quarters to welcome the New Year in a worthy fashion. Unfortunately, I can't be part of the celebrations much longer because the lookout on deck is waiting to be relieved. I am getting ready to take over the watch. Coming on deck, I hear the Flak shooting from several locations on shore greeting the New Year with fireworks and to make sure it doesn't start too quietly.

Taking over the watch, I wish my comrade who was at the post until now a happy New Year because judging from all the noise that comes from the deck below I assume that it is now midnight. The lookouts from the Infantry and the Flak come over to exchange New Year's greetings. The comrades down in the living deck haven't forgotten their watchman either. Many are coming up to wish me a happy New Year. But it doesn't take long and I am alone again. I hear them singing from below. After a while all falls silent below, my buddies went to sleep. In the ensuing silence, I am thinking back to home. It was just a year ago that I celebrated the New Year with my parents. I wasn't in the military yet. My greatest wish at that time was to get to the Front where the action was. Now I am here and I am proud of it.

Wed. Jan. 1, 1941

Reveille is at 0830. The crew rolled out of their hammocks more tired than usual. But New Year happens only once. After the customary potato peeling and ship cleaning, we received our military pay and cigarettes.

In the afternoon I went ashore for the first time to explore the city of Lorient.

Thur. Jan. 2

Getting on deck this morning it looked like winter had arrived. It snowed here for the first time. The holidays are over and it is back to work. Beginning today I am assigned to lookout duty under the

15

Signal Chief. At 1030, following "clean sweep-down fore and aft", we are ready to depart. After leaving the pier, I am assigned to the maneuver station to boatswain mate Traumitz who explained to us the handling of the (mooring) lines. Leaving port we encounter a strong, icy wind blowing 6 to 7 (Beaufort scale) all day long.

Fri. Jan. 3

Today we are introduced to signals and Morse codes followed by "Behavior on Board". After taking care of personal belongings, I begin the battle station watch at 1600 Soon thereafter we anchor at "our island" (Isle of Groix). After my watch from midnight to 0200, my day finally ends. We also learned in boatswain mate Ramen's class about lines and soundings. Following this, we have Flak exercise under Ltn. Schmidt. At 1400, we practice shooting for the first time, beginning with the 2-cm (gun). Because of the unfavorable position of the balloon we couldn't shoot until the balloon was a distance away. Therefore we did not hit it. But the shots were pretty close. The 3.7cm took a balloon down. Generally the shooting results were satisfying.

Figure 16 My maneuver station

Sat. Jan.4

We weighed anchor at 0930. Boatswain's mate Schmidt lectured about sea lane rules. Ltn. Wilke explained the construction of our Sperrbrecher. At 1230, we arrived in our port and tied up pierside. At 1600, we lined up on deck for an inspection by Captain Jakob. After that, I went on shore leave with Dietz and Hans.

Figure 17 Harbor entrance of Lorient

Mon. Jan. 6

Today we are staying in port. In the morning we have a lesson on position-keeping and blockade. In the afternoon, we have signal and infantry duty. The latter was taught by boatswain's mate Albrecht. Since we were trained with the Karabiner 98K it was somehow unfamiliar to use a 98 rifle. But it was fun, because since we left Stralsund we didn't have any infantry duty. Afterwards we cleaned our rifles.

Tues. Jan. 7

At 0930, we are ready to go to sea. It snowed again and we had to sweep the snow off the deck. When we reached open water, we stowed the lines and then had a lesson in splicing and knots. When we got on deck at 1030, we discovered that we were escorting a U-boat out. It followed about 500m back in our wake. A lively Morse exchange took place between us and the U-boat. After sufficient distance from the harbor entrance and the island, a red flag was waved to the port side. We turned around toward port and the U-boat continued on its own now. We barely had turned around when a second U-boat appeared, guided by two patrol vessels. We exchanged greetings with blink signals. After that we proceeded alone. At 1400, we were singing on the port berthing deck. It was followed with Flak C distance reckoning and after that a short discussion about ammunition. We went on anchor at 1730.

Figure 18 We escorted a U-boat out.   **Figure 19 Our flag on the mast**
Now it goes on its own power

Wed. Jan. 8

Today, from 0930 to 1020, we learned about Morse procedures followed by applied navigation. In the afternoon we talked about fog and sound signals. We cleaned our personal belongings for the remainder of the afternoon. This was really necessary because our stuff is anything but clean.

Thur. Jan. 9

We got underway at 0930. Today we are learning about command transmissions together with seaman Fritze at the front with the earphones on. Following this, Ltn. Schoenfelder takes us into the engine room. This was very interesting to me because years back, my father had taken me to several technical plants and therefore I had no problem with most of the things (we were shown). After a quick lunch we had watch until 1400.

From 1400-1600, we had nautical lessons. We talked about anchors, how to hoist and launch life boats. The last thing was "clean deck" for all of us.

Figure 20 11 marks were on the bridge when we came on board. Now there are 14. Each mark means one mine.

The 9th of January was special day for us. At 1300, we detonated our 3rd mine while we were standing at the signal deck. When we first came on board there were 11 black marks painted on the bridge. Today there are already 14.

Fri. Jan. 10

We had signal duty all morning long, first signaling from the ship's deck then blink signals from the crew deck followed by watch until 1230. From 1400-1600, we had navigations lessons. At 1730, we returned pierside. I was surprised how many Christmas packages had arrived. I had already given up on them.

Sat. Jan. 11

Today, the Captain taught a lesson about Service Procedures. First we talked about battle stations and the roles everybody has. It's unbelievable how quickly one becomes awake when having to climb three times over the masthead. Seaman Henne can attest to that. After a short break we had a navigation class with Ltn. Wilke. At 1130 we had to report on deck. The captain awarded 15 min sweeping medals. I am not going ashore today. Instead I will answer my mail.

Sun. Jan. 12

At 1130 we have Corporal inspection. Starting today we have a fixed duty plan. The port watch had shore leave. Air raid alarm sounded in the evening. Four bombs fell at the railway station in Lorient.

Figure 21 Our 3.7 cm gun

Mon. Jan. 13

We had a Seamanship lesson with boatswain's mate Meetschen. We made a knot line and a Becket Bend on a towing hawser for mooring or towing. That took us all afternoon. For the first time we practiced on the 3.7cm cannon. I am number 6; that is the right- side loading number. When everything goes according to plan, these practices can be fun. We had to rush to the quarterdeck a couple of times. The boatswain's mate didn't want to be slower than us but he wasn't as flexible anymore as we were. In the rush he smashed his head into the bulkhead with the result that he got a big bump on his forehead. Air raid warnings were given in the evening but nothing special happened.

Tues. Jan. 14

At 1100, we left port. Our section had signal duty until 1130. The sending and decoding of blink signals is still very slow. It still takes about 15 minutes to transmit a short text. But with time and practice we will learn this too. The afternoon lesson is on rendering honors on board. It was followed by a lesson on Ship Logs and Soundings. Returning to the signal deck at 1635 for underway watch we blew up our 4th mine, which means another mark on the bridge. So far our ship has rendered 15 mines useless. Going on anchor in the evening we had a half hour lesson in astronomy and with the help of a sextant "we plucked the stars from the sky". Finally after finishing my 0200 to 0400 watch, the day was over for me.

Wed. Jan. 15

We have detailed role duty. We start at 1000. After certain signals the "all men into the lifeboats and on the floats" command is given. "Fire in ship, man overboard, clear ship and air raid warning". Because of dense fog we go on anchor at 1250.

At 1300, we weighed anchor. During our on-board PE around 1900, the ship started to shake violently. Boatswain's mate Meetschen bolts to one side. Immediately a water column rises at starboard . First it's shallow but then it rises higher and higher until it reaches its peak and collapses in itself again leaving only a boiling, stinking funnel. This was my 5th mine, for the ship #16. Following this we take care of our personal belongings. We tie up at pierside in the evening.

Figure 22 Boom, our 5th mine explodes.

Thur. Jan. 16

At 0930, we are clear to go to sea. Boatswain's mate Meetschen inspects our lockers before the lesson on the 3.7 cm SKC 30. It's a disaster. I think we got it now that the 3.7 cm SKC 30 is a twin barreled Flak gun, 30 cal, with a three axial arrangement. The next class dealt again with how to hoist and launch a lifeboat. After the navigation class and signal duty, we went on anchor. We had to report on deck with packed sea bags because of our poor performance during the morning locker inspection. But even this will pass. After we put all our belongings back into the lockers and boatswain's mate Meetschen had intensively scrutinized them, this thing was finally over.

Fri. Jan. 17

In Signal class, we learned the significance of the flags. This took the entire morning. In the afternoon we had infantry duty. The army soldiers are lucky that they don't have to do that under the same condition because it is not easy on a rolling ship. Each of us was put in command of the whole group once. Shortly before the end of this exercise, the ship was shaken by a strong blast. We had blown up our 17th mine. It's our lucky week because it doesn't happen often to render a mine useless almost every day. After that, the Chief Machinist Mate demonstrated the flood and pump equipment of our ship. A short time later we tied up pierside, but this time not on the starboard side. We are learning the reason for this the next day.

Sat. Jan. 18

Today we are getting our 3. 7cm portside cannon back and our ship looks totally different. After the normal duty we are in for a joyous surprise. We put the ship's launch in the water and practiced take-offs and landings under boatswain's mate Ramen. We were especially happy when the control was handed to us and we had the command of the boat.

Figure 23 The M.P. at backboard

In the afternoon we had some time to ourselves. I did my laundry. I couldn't go on shore since I had watch duty.

Sun. Jan. 19

At 1100, we lined up on the ship deck for muster. In the afternoon my buddies and I went ashore. We went to the movies and saw "Kleider machen Leute". We couldn't show off our uniforms because we were surprised by a rain shower and were drenched by the time we returned aboard.

Mon. Jan. 20

At 0930, we were on our way. The sea was rough today. We had a class about the anchors and their equipment. Because the ship was rolling severely it didn't take long for some men to pay Neptune their tribute. More and more were leaving to render their sacrifice. In the end only three of us remained (in class). Since the others did not return the class was cancelled. When we finally got up on deck, several (poor souls) were hanging over the railing and couldn't live or die. Although I felt pity for them I had to laugh. But the best remedy against seasickness is fresh air and work. Therefore we put the lifelines across the deck. In the afternoon we practiced on the 3.7 cm. Once in a while we were interrupted by the ones who had to pay their tribute to Neptune in installments. We anchored at 1700, and I am certain that some of us were glad they could crawl into their hammocks now. I still have watch from 0200 to 0400, and then this day is over.

Tues. Jan. 21

We had signal duty all morning. At 1230, we went on Battle Station watch. Today we hit good luck again. At 1547 we cracked our 18th and my 7th mine. It exploded port side. Between 1400 and 1500, we practiced applied logging, first with the reeling log line and then with the patent log. The results between the two differed slightly, but taking the middle value of the two determined our true speed. The next class was "Rendering Honors on Board". We just didn't get it and were relieved when we were released after an hour.

Wed. Jan 22

We went to sea at 0930. Between 1000 and 1130, we were assigned to play certain roles. As ill luck will have it we had to bring the break-down notes to the different stations.

Because of bad weather, we spent the afternoon with clean-up duty followed by PE. I had signal watch from 0200 until 0400.

Figure 24 Airplane 180 degree, Aim

Figure 25 Stop Battery

Thur. Jan. 23

Despite the hard rain this morning we had artillery practice. Then we went to the living deck and took the breech apart.

In the afternoon class with boatswain's mate Ramen we learned about the magnetic compass. It was followed by the signal class and where we learned which flags represented the letters "A"," Ä", "B", "C" and "D". When we returned to the pier at 5:15 PM the mooring line broke. It snapped like a bungee cord.

Fri. Jan 24

We had Morse code and signaling practice all morning long followed by infantry duty in the afternoon. Even on the small pier area we were working up a sweat. It was followed by "Ship Knowledge" and we talked about the anchor equipment of our ship followed by a walk throughout the whole ship.

Figure 26 The spill and the anchor chains

Sat. Jan.25

This morning we have "Service Knowledge" with the captain. We talked about how to place a complaint. It was followed by Navigation with Ltn. Wilke. We talked about celestial navigation. I still don't understand this completely.

I went to the theater in the afternoon. A KDF (Kraft durch Freude - the equivalent of USO) played music by Mozart. In the evening I went to the movie "Hurra, ich bin ein Papa". It was funny.

Figure 27 A U-boat comes back

Figure 28 "Mine" our board dog

Sun. January 26

In the morning the captain inspected the ship. After that we lined up at the "Wicklung" (location of the mine detection gear) for muster. Later I took care of my mail. The rest of the time I spent with "Mine", our board dog.

Mon. Jan. 27

I was on the front deck for the departure maneuver. We worked with the knot line. During artillery duty we learned about the first malfunctioning problems. We dropped anchor at 1800.

Tues. Jan. 28

At 0915, we weighed anchor. Afternoon classes were Navigation and Duty Knowledge. Boatswain's mate Meetschen inspected the lockers. It's difficult with such limited space available to satisfy the critical eyes of the boatswain mate. We still have problems with "Rendering Honors on Board". Therefore we wrote everything down in the hope that we will do it correctly now.

But today, after all the writing, Fortune smiled at us. My 8th mine exploded. By now our ship blew up 19 mines. In the evening we docked pierside.

Wed. Jan. 29

Due to dense fog we stayed in port. The district commander visited the ship today. But this was interrupted since "special assignment" was called for the whole ship. I was on the signal deck on the telephone. For the remainder of the morning we were on artillery duty again. Two guys who did not know the malfunctioning procedures had to write a "love letter" to the boatswain's mate. From 1330 to 1430, we had sport ashore where we played handball. In the end, the ball fell into the water, but we had a brave rescuer and with the help of the gangway plank and a boat hook we were able to fish it out again. At 1530 we went out to sea. We had clean-up duty for our personal stuff. I did my laundry. We anchored at 1930.

Thur. Jan. 30

At 0915, we weighed anchor. We have a lesson on "Seamanship" with Schmadding (deck master). Learning knots and splices in his class is great. In the afternoon after the Navigation class we had Signal Recognition class.

At 1730, we docked at the pier. While we were tying up, two U-boats and a minesweeper were going out. With hand signals we wished them a happy journey.

Fri. Jan. 31

While ashore, we were practicing signaling with signaling discs followed by Morse code. In the afternoon we had drill instructions.

But today we were not alone on our small drill field. We were joined by the signal men. This was followed by a class about the ship's engines.

Sat., Feb.1

This morning we had boat duty. The cutter is tied to the deck of the ship with a small line that can be quickly removed. Boatswain's mate Meetschen showed us the basics of towing making a lot of noise doing so. This wasn't new for me since we learned to pull at the NPEA Oranienstein. I was glad when we finally let go of the ship and puttered around in port. At the end, we hoisted the boat back on board and tied it down. We loaded provisions early in the afternoon. The rest of the afternoon was left to us. I had to iron my trousers.

Sun. Feb.2

Today was a typical Sunday routine. At 1130 was muster. In the afternoon some friends and I went to the film "Anton der Letzte".

Mon. Feb 3

We were ready to sail at 0930. In class we learned about knots and splices with Schmadding. Then we moved to the deck and practiced coiling and heaving lines. I now have a new Battle Station position. I am Assistant Helmsman. Steering is fun. In the beginning, the ship ran away from me a couple of times. But then I mastered it. In the afternoon we had practice on the 3.7 cm gun, followed by some theory lessons. I had watch from 1400 to 1600.

Tues. Feb.4

We weighed anchor at 0915. In the morning we had signal duty. While on watch I was the Assistant Helmsman. In the afternoon we talked about meteorology. It was followed by "Rendering Honors on Board". We docked at the pier at 1715, and Fritz and I went into town. I finally finished my laundry.

Wed. Feb. 5

We spent the morning artillery duty in. Boatswain's mate Meetschen made us run across the ship a couple of times. We set sail in the afternoon. Today we made an exciting moving maneuver but we got out of the harbor alright. Ltn. Merkel is the division officer of the starboard watch. Today I was relieved from my post as helmsman and I am now participating in Navigation. PE in the afternoon was canceled. We brought our logbooks up to date, and cleaned up our personal belongings. We anchored at 1700.

Figure 29 The Captain on the bridge

Thur. Feb. 6

I had the watch from 0400 to 0800. We weighed anchor already at 0600 and left under the cover of darkness. We oriented ourselves on the blinking lights of the lighthouse. In addition we sailed after tide and soundings. For this we had to calculate the strength of the current and the wind velocity. We had a seamanship lesson with Schmadding. In the afternoon after the underway watch we had Navigation class by helms mate Baum. We worked with the sextant. This was followed by a class about signaling with flags. In the staff master's opinion we are not fast enough.

When we returned to port I received the joyous news that I have become an uncle. I am as proud as my beloved little sister, the happy mother. I just regret that it is not a boy. Despite this it's my pleasure to become little Frauke's godfather.

Fri. Feb.7

To our big surprise we went out to sea today. We had signal duty in the morning. Infantry duty was canceled. After returning to port we had a lesson about the effects of rudder and screw.

Sat. Feb.8

In the morning we had ship duty and we cruised around in the harbor. In the afternoon I went into Lorient.

Sun. Feb.9

We went on a march today. It was nice to get the kinks out of the legs. Afterwards the ferry brought us back aboard.

Figure 30 1st Division lined up at the Wicklung for muster

Mon. Feb.10

We were on the bridge during the departure maneuver. The captain explained rudder and propeller effects. Following this we learned knotting and splicing of heavy ropes. This is different from working with the lighter ropes. I was the navigation student during the Battle Station watch. In the afternoon we had artillery duty on the 3.7 cm gun. At 1815 we dropped anchor at "our" island (Isle of Groix).

Figure 31 Muster by the captain

Tue. Feb.11

We were supposed to weigh anchor at 0915. But because of very dense fog we stayed put all morning. We had signal duty. We practiced transmitting short paragraphs from the newspaper in Morse code. In the afternoon navigation class with helms mate Baum we talked about sea lane markers, beaconing, dead reckoning and the compass. This was followed by Duty Knowledge with boatswain mate Meetschen. It was foggy again during Battle Station watch; therefore it was difficult to take soundings. We returned to port in the evening and docked pierside.

Wed. Feb.12

We sailed at 0915. At 1000, we assembled on deck for role duty. During this "all hands" exercise we had artillery duty. The afternoon sport was canceled because of rain. In its place the captain taught a lesson on the significance of marine codes. It was followed by clean-up duty. The starboard watch was off duty today. We anchored at 1815.

Figure 32 The long swells of the Atlantic

Thur. Feb. 13

We weighed anchor at 0915. Today was a special day. For the first time we practiced sharp shooting with the 3.7 cm. When the first balloon rose, the 2 cm opened fire. After the balloon was too far away for the 2 cm, the 3.7 cm was supposed to get permission to fire but the lights suddenly went out and we were unable to open fire. The other guns had problems too. The gun crews had to line up on deck and were reprimanded. Then we returned to the guns. This time things went better.

Figure 33 The 2cm ready for firing

The tension slowly dissipated when we finally got to fire. I fired shot after shot from the right barrel. For me everything went without a glitch. It happened once that the recoil wasn't strong enough and the closure breech did not open. I just opened it by hand as we had learned in practice. In the beginning the left barrel had a lot of problems. But in the end everything was working. Unfortunately I couldn't see how accurate the shots were since I had to concentrate on my barrel.

Part of our gun crew had to clean the guns. Our 20th mine exploded during our navigation and signal duty and my company got credit for nine. At the end of the day we sailed around the whole island (Isle of Groix.) The west side looks bare and rocky. We passed Fort Louis (at the entrance of the harbor of Lorient) and returned to the pier.

We learned by special announcement that an enemy convoy had been attacked. 14 ships were sunk. This is a devastating blow for England.

Figure 34 The distances are transmitted from the E-instrument to the batteries

Figure 35 cleaning gun

Figure 36 Fort Louis

Fri. Feb.14

After "clean ship" we had signal duty. First we talked about the layout of the signal book and the meaning of the flags and auxiliary signals. Then we sent newspaper paragraphs by Morse code. During the second hour we went on pier to practice hand signaling. In the afternoon we updated our log books and took care of our personal stuff.

Figure 37 The bow of our ship

Sat. Feb.15

During the morning we practiced operating the ship's launch. Afterwards we changed clothes and lined up for muster. It was a special day for part of the crew because they are awarded the EKII (Iron Cross 2nd Class). I was put in charge of the launch in the afternoon. We brought the liberty detail ashore. It was a quiet afternoon without any incidents. When night fell things didn't go as planned. It was so dark that the visibility was reduced to less than 20 m. It took some time until we found the entrance to the district command.

Then, at our last departure from shore, the engine of the launch did not start. We waited until 0200 before we got off the launch to look for accommodations for the rest of the night. Seaman Greulich and I were asked to go to the pier and inform our ship of our mishap. We were given a strong flashlight with which we were supposed to try sending a Morse message.

Sending Morse signals to our ship a replay was sent immediately. We now transmitted our whole sermon. We got a R.P. (Romeo Papa or Read again, transmission was indecipherable) from the other side. When we came to the middle of the message we again received a R.P. again but finally everything worked. We were informed that a line had broken and that they planned to launch a cutter since the launch wasn't operational. A motor pool car picked us up and brought us to the arsenal. A tugboat returned us to our ship. To our great surprise our launch was also back on board and obviously repaired again. The broken line turned out to be less serious than we thought. Only the tiller was broken. This damage too was quickly fixed.

We went straight into our hammocks because by now it was past 0330.

Figure 38 2 tugboats guide us to the anchoring buoy

Sun. Feb. 16

Today is Sunday routine. In the afternoon I went ashore with seaman Fritze and we saw the film "Hotel Sacher".

Figure 39 A minesweeper is leaving

Mon. Feb. 17

At 0915, we were ready for departure. We had "Seamanship" by Schmadding. In the afternoon we had artillery duty followed by locker inspection.

Figure 40 On search cruise

Tues. Feb. 18

After weighing anchor we had signal duty followed by a navigation class in the afternoon. After that our personal belongings were inspected.

Figure 41 We are meeting a scout boat

Wed. Feb.19

We had artillery duty in the morning. At noon we had to anchor because the generator failed. Since we couldn't repair it we returned to port. In the afternoon seaman Greulich and I drove the launch. At 2300 after we had tied up at the ship air the raid alarm sounded. But we didn't spot any airplanes. Therefore we were sent back to our bunks.

Figure 42 We detonated our 20th mine

Thur. Feb. 20

We took the ship's launch out in the morning and practiced landing and buoy maneuvers. In the afternoon Navigation class we turned the radio direction finder on and searched for stations. It was followed by manual signal practice during signal duty class.

Fri. Feb. 21

We were operating the launch all morning long. The captain himself observed our maneuvering skills. In the afternoon I was in charge (of the launch) bringing the Chief Signal Master and boatswain's mate Meetschen ashore.

Sat. Feb. 22

In the morning we operated the launch again. At noon we cut loose from the anchoring buoy and tied-up at the pier. Because it was raining again, as usual when we are off watch, we had to wear our oilcloths to go ashore. We saw the film "Mutterliebe". After doing some shopping we returned aboard.

Figure 43 The heaving line flies to land

Sun. Feb.23

I had to stay on board because I had watch. That gave me lot of time to get my things in order and to answer all my mail.

14 days of machine duty

Mon. Feb.24

We started our machine activities today. I was so disappointed to have Ex-duty in the morning. (Extra duty an additional watch normally given because some task that should have or did not get done). But in the afternoon we got going. I am assigned to the auxiliary diesel engine. I am learning how to lubricate the diesel and how to regulate the cooling system. We were told what role the auxiliary diesel plays. This duty is tiring and I was glad when I got into the fresh air again. I had watch from 0020 until 0300.

Tues. Feb. 25

I had a hard time getting up in the morning. But after half an hour of sport I was up to speed again. In the afternoon it was back to the engine room and the auxiliary diesel. At 6 PM we returned to the pier. I had the watch from midnight until 0400.

Wed. Feb. 26

We were going out to sea at 0900. Since I didn't have any duty, I had time to do my laundry during the morning. In the afternoon I was assigned to Generator II. This duty didn't last long since we were returning to port at 1400. We had to get ready for muster. The captain congratulated us on our promotion to sea cadets. At 1700, the whole crew lined up on deck. We were inspected by the Chief of the III Security Division. He addressed us, the newly appointed sea cadets. Afterwards I went ashore with Gernot and Ekki to celebrate our promotion. Returning to the ship we had to report to the Ward room where the other comrades were already celebrating the promotion. We celebrated until midnight before we retired to our hammocks.

Thur. Feb.27

I had watch from 0800 until 1230. We checked the main engine. The afternoon was spent with clean-up duty. In the evening I was on watch from 2000 until midnight.

Fri. Feb. 28

In the morning we had to clean the engine room. At 1300 was mustered on the on the sweep deck where the minesweeping gear is located in large spools of wire . The Chief of the Flotilla conducted the inspection and he briefly talked to the crew.

Later in the afternoon we went to the movies and saw "Der Tag nach der Scheidung".

Sat. Mar. 1

During the morning I had to sweep the crew quarters. Then I had the watch from noon until 1600. Unfortunately I also had the middle watch during the night.

Sun. Mar. 2

No inspection this morning. In the afternoon I went ashore with Fritze and Ekki and we met our former classmates from Stralsund. This turned into a big party.

Mon. Mar. 3

We had to get up at 0600. At 0630, we climbed down to the engine room. I spent the whole morning lubricating the diesel, washing the paint and cleaning tools. A diver was deployed to work on the driveshaft seal. At 1700, we launched the ship's launch to the Isle of Groix with the liberty detail on board.

Tues. Mar. 4

We took the exhaust valves out of the auxiliary diesel 1 today. I spent all my time taking the valves apart, cleaning, polishing and reassembling them. In the future no auto mechanic needs show me how to do this. In the afternoon we took care of our personal stuff. After that I was on watch from 1830 until 2130. Then the day was over for me.

Wed. Mar. 5

Today was role duty. We didn't see much of it down here in the engine room. At one time we had to get back on deck because of a leak. But it was fixed quickly and we could return. We went on anchor at 1800.

Thur. Mar. 6

Today I cleaned valves again. But Fritze took over. I then cleaned the oil purifier. We docked at 1600. I had the watch from 1600 until 2000.

Fri. Mar. 7

We had engine duty in the morning and changed the fuel valves. I had to take the used ones apart, clean and reassemble them. At 1600, Gernot and I went ashore. He did not like the local mineral water at all.

Sat. Mar. 8

Today was our last day in the engine room. Together with Grosser, I took the main engine's lubricant and cooling oil filters apart and cleaned them.

After dinner I went ashore with Gernot and we went to the movies and watched "Aus erster Ehe". It was very heroic.

Sun. Mar. 9

As usual when we are on leave it was raining. At 1100, we had to report for muster. We were told that we will get leave in about two weeks. This was great news for us. Starting today Ltn. Merkle is cadet officer. In the afternoon I had my picture taken by a photographer.

Mon. Mar. 10

We were back on deck today and began with PE and then had a lesson in "Seamanship" with boatswain's mate Meetschen. Knots are our favorite subject because we can do them pretty well. We were signalmen on the Battle Station watch. In the afternoon we practiced on the 2 cm artillery.

We went on anchor at 1730, not at our usual location but further out. From there we had the luck to go with the launch ashore to visit the ship's summer home. It's in a beautiful place, the ideal place for R and R. We returned to the ship at 2000.

Tues. Mar. 11

After the morning PE, we had signal duty with the staff signal master. We hadn't forgotten too much during our time in the engine room. We actually did pretty well. We practiced hand signals during the Battle Station watch. The beautiful sunshine today made the on-deck duty fun.

Wed. Mar. 12

We weighed anchor during our morning PE. We had artillery duty until 1000. While on Battle Station watch, Ltn. Merkle explained the EU and 9V. This was followed by a Fire Control practice during which we had to calibrate the instruments. In the afternoon we had PE again followed by cleaning our personal stuff. We anchored at 17:17 PM.

Thur. Mar. 13

At 0830 during our morning PE, we weighted anchor. We spent the rest of the morning with signal duty and the afternoon classes with Morse and Navigation. We worked on sea charts and calculated the deviation of the compass through soundings.

Fri. Mar. 14

We just can't imagine the day without the morning PE. Following that we took the flak gun apart and got a lesson on that.

The normal routine for the afternoon was canceled. Everybody not on duty went to the athletic field. We played a great handball match, which resembled the American football. We were on the winning team. Even boatswain's mate Meetschen, who played a great defense, couldn't spoil our victory. Ltn. Schönfelder was awarded the EK1 (Iron Cross 1st class). Later a naval clergyman talked to us about the economical background of this war. After that we all enjoyed the sunshine.

Sat. Mar. 15

Today we boarded the cutter and puttered around in the harbor. We were dismissed at 1100. After lunch we went on an excursion. We took the train to the little town of Auray which is noticeably cleaner and more attractive than Lorient. Regrettably we had to return after 2 hours.

I was in my bunk when the air raid alarm sounded. We all had to get on deck. As usual the Tommies dropped target flares, one right above our ship. But the Flak shot it down with a well aimed shot. Several bombs fell. Our searchlight engulfed one large airplane (Lancaster bomber). But despite an intensive Flak barrage it wasn't shot down. After that everything was quiet again.

Sun. Mar. 16

Today, Heroes Remembrance Day, we dressed the ship. At 1100, we lined up for muster. After that we all listened to a speech by the Führer (Adolf Hitler).

In the afternoon I went ashore to do some shopping. It was then that I saw the result of the British bombing raid. One house was destroyed. The other bombs fell into a pasture and one on a street intersection. We returned aboard with a pretty flower bouquet.

Mon. Mar. 17

After the morning PE we had artillery duty on the 2 cm. The afternoon class was about Seamanship. After that we launched the cutter, raised the sail and sailed until the ship anchored.

Tues. Mar. 18

Today we tied up at the pier. In the afternoon we had shore leave. I stayed aboard to take care of my mail. At 1700, the captain delivered the good news that we are going on leave.

Wed. Mar. 19

In the morning we handed in our material and packed our suitcases. Our train left at 2030.

(15 days of leave follow during which time SPERRBRECHER 1 was moved to Brest for repair).

Fri. Apr. 4

Our train arrived in Brest at noon. We barely were on board and had opened our suitcases when boatswain's mate Meetschen spotted us. "Ah, here are our gentlemen cadets. Hurry up and get changed, vacations are over. I want to see you in 5 minutes in tackle dress on deck." That was our welcome.

In the afternoon we hauled about 1000 bottles of beer aboard. When the other boatswain's mates spotted us they all had work for us to do. After our regular work we emptied and cleaned the kitchen refuse barrels. Afterwards we got to see the ship from underneath because it was in the dry dock.

In the evening, I had just retired to my hammock when the air raid alarm was sounded. The Tommies tried to welcome us to Brest. They didn't visit us so often in Lorient because it was further away for them.

We got our excitement. One bomb fell into a nearby railroad tanker car and set it ablaze. That gave the Tommies a good target marker. Nine bombs dropped near us on the east pier. Some of our crew unhooked the remaining tanker cars from the burning one and pushed them away to avoid an even bigger explosion. In the meantime a Tommy flew a low level attack and showered us with machine gun salvos. But the plane was a good target for our guns also. We fired from all barrels. All in all three airplanes were shot down during the attack.

Sat. Apr. 5

Duty commenced as listed in the duty plan. Because of the bad weather I did not go ashore today.

Sun. Apr. 6

First air raid alarm sounded at 0800. More followed throughout the day.

During the muster, the captain issued a citation for our action during the night from April 4-5. We were credited with one downing (of an airplane). We also found out that the battleship GNEISENAU was attacked by a torpedo bomber and was hit.

In the afternoon we learned that German troops have entered Yugoslavia and Greece. Finally we are making progress over there.

48

Mon. Apr. 7

In the morning we drove the launch. The GNEISENAU is already in the dry dock (for repair). In the afternoon we had the first practice shooting with the 10.5 cm gun. Later in the day, Otto and I picked up the Master Sergeant's suitcase from the railway station. We didn't return to the ship (on time) because we were supposed to pick up eggs for Shipmate Pröpper and we were chided for this by the Master Sergeant.

Tues. Apr. 8

We had signal duty in the morning, first hand signaling then by Morse signals.

In the afternoon we have Navigation and Service Knowledge classes.

Wed. Apr. 9

Muster at 0930 on the ship deck. The captain read the citation by the Chief of the 3rd Safety Division, Captain Schiller, for our outstanding action during the April 4 bombing raid.

After that we had signal duty, first Morse signaling followed by flag signaling.

By afternoon the drydock was fully flooded and we were getting ready for departure. We were sailing until 2000 and then anchored at the anchorage.

Thur. Apr. 10

We weighed anchor at 0800 in the morning. We had watch on the bridge. After PE we had a class about Seamanship by Schmadding. In the afternoon we launched the ship's launch. At 1400, we continued our cruise.

In the afternoon we had Navigation class by boatswain mate Kamm followed by signal duty. At 2030, we dropped anchor at the harbor entrance.

At 2100, an air raid warning was sounded. The Tommies dropped a multitude of bombs. But today we had hunter's luck. One Tommy approached very low. When he was about 200 m away our 3.7 cm and 2 cm guns started firing. The first shots were already great. The plane caught fire, turned away and crashed into a forest.

After the alarm was canceled I had signal watch and therefore I stayed right on deck.

Fri. Apr. 11

Since we had to get up a couple of times during the night we were allowed to sleep in this morning. Duty was canceled also. We only went on Battle Station watch. We escorted a buoy tender out of the harbor. At about 1700, we blew up our 22nd mine. Shortly thereafter the LÜNEBURG also blew up a mine. We are here in Brest with five other Sperrbrechers. Also the battleships SCHARNHORST and GNEISENAU are here with some patrol vessels and minesweepers.

Sat. Apr. 12

At 0800, we were ready to sail, followed by the normal routine and a lecture by the captain about the effects of alcohol and narcotics. Then we talked about Identification signals followed by a Navigation class.

While returning in the afternoon and searching for a place to anchor, a mine exploded immediately beside the ship and near the port driveshaft. We had a lot of damage on board. The engine failed briefly but later we were able to go on anchor.

Sun. Apr. 13, Easter

The outstanding food let us know that it was Easter. In the afternoon I and three of my comrades went ashore and explored the peninsula (Crozon). The steep bluffs were especially beautiful. Flowers were blooming everywhere. We noticed the vast expanses of Thorny Scott's Brush with its beautiful yellow blossoms. The locals are using it as firewood. Returning from Roscanvel in the evening we were rightfully chided because some of the fellows had looked too deep into a glass.

Mon. Apr. 14, Easter (Easter is a two day holiday in Germany)

Wake-up call at 0730. At 0800, we weighed anchor. All morning we were waiting for the buoy tender, but because of some propeller damage it didn't come. Therefore we departed alone. We dropped anchor at 1730.

I had been in my hammock for just an hour in the evening when air raid alarm was given. The intended target seemed to be the GNEISENAU because several bombs were dropped nearby. Four bombs actually hit the GNEISENAU which resulted in over 100 fatalities. The Tommies heavily damaged the city itself also. Fires were burning in several places and rows of houses were destroyed. We could not fire because the planes flew too high. The alarm lasted until 0600.

Tues. Apr. 15

Spending the whole night outside we were allowed to sleep-in in the morning. Duty was also canceled. When we left the harbor we were joined by SPERRBRECHER 36. It followed in our wake. We did a lot of signaling forth and back. During the changing of the watch and while on our way down (into the ship) our 24th mine blew up at 1600. We dropped anchor at 2000.

Wed. Apr. 16

Today we "shot" the sun and the moon and calculated our position. In the afternoon we had to cleanup our personal stuff. We anchored at 1800.
At noon we detonated our jubilee mine: #25. To celebrate the occasion we were served punch in the evening.

Thur. Apr. 17

The day began with PE followed by artillery duty. At the moment when we were walking to the front of the U-boat and torpedo boat gun, the ship was shaken by a tremendous explosion. A mine had gone up directly beneath us. We had a lot of damage on the vessel.

51

Because both engines failed we were forced to drop anchor. Later we were able to restart one engine and with that we moved to the anchorage and anchored.

In the afternoon we still had our navigation class and worked on our damaged echo-sounding and direction finder. This was followed by flag signaling.

Fri. Apr. 18

In the morning the starboard watch was off and had gone ashore because we docked pierside at 0800. At 1200 was muster. All of us, except Ekki, got the minesweeper medals. That served Ekki right.

In the afternoon we loaded ammunition and provisions. At 2000 we anchored at the anchorage.

Sat. Apr. 19

We docked pierside at 0800. We then set the launch out. We were off duty in the afternoon.

Sun. Apr. 20

0700 wake-up call. In honor of the Führer's Birthday we dressed ship. We then left for open water. Since we were going far out we went with an escort. At 1042, we detonated our 27th mine and at1545 PM # 28. Then we returned to the anchorage. After lowering the launch, Fritze and I were in charge of it. We went to the island to pick up our liberty detail.

Mon. Apr. 21

Because of some leaking sea valves we are not going to sea today. After our morning PE we had a Seamanship lesson. We cleared the lock rods on the lifeboats, swung the gangway out and painted the ship. We had artillery service in the afternoon. After that we went sailing with Ltn. Merkle.

Tues. Apr. 22

After our exercise we had signal duty. We learned about interference, hand and light signals. Early in the afternoon we had a

Navigation lesson. The rest of the afternoon I went sailing with Ekki, boatswain's mate Meetschen and our fireman.

Wed. Apr. 23

We went into the dry dock today. We got new role assignments. In the afternoon we had to clean-up our stuff and get ready for our trip to Paris. We left the ship at 1800 together with Ltn. Merkle and boatswain's mate Meetschen. To shorten the boring overnight train trip we played Skat [a popular German card game].

Thurs. Apr. 24

We arrived in Paris at 0630 and went to the city commandant to get our IDs and housing assignments. Then we walked to our hotel. After we cleaned up we had a good breakfast. Shortly thereafter Ltn. Merkle arrived with three sedans and we set out to explore Paris. In the evening we all went to the Faborin [night club].

Figure 44 Eiffel Tower

Fri. Apr. 25

When I woke up in the morning the others were already at breakfast. I quickly caught up with them. We got in our cars and drove to

Versailles. Unfortunately it was raining and storming and walking around was no fun. By the time we returned to Paris we had gotten a good overview of the city. Our city guide went all out to show us the most beautiful parts. He also knew little anecdotes and stories about the things he was showing us. It wasn't always historically correct, but then it came from the French point of view which wasn't always the same as ours. At Versailles I was strongly reminded of the NPEA Oranienstein, (his military prep school that was housed in Castle Oranienstein) although our school wasn't as lavishly appointed. But the ceiling plasterwork and the artworks were a strong reminder. In the evening I went with Hansi to the Chez Elle [night club]. There we met boatswain's mates Lüders and Doerz. It was a beautifully relaxing evening. Our leave ended 2300 and therefore we had to leave before the end (of the performance) to catch the Metro back home. Today was much more expensive than yesterday.

Figure 45 Grave of the unknown soldier

Figure 46 Arc de Triomphe

Sat. Apr. 26

It's our last day in Paris. We were given the whole day to ourselves. In the morning I went to a military library and bought some books.

Then we did some shopping and had a fancy lunch. In the evening I went with Hänschen to the Lido [night club]. Again we had to leave early since our curfew arrived too soon. It was a nice finale for Paris.

Figure 47 Tomb of Napoleon I and Dome des Invalides

Figure 48 Tomb of Marshall Foch

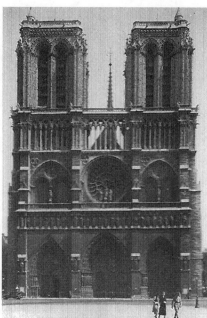

Figure 49 Sacre Coeur and Basilica Notre Dame Cathedral

Sun. Apr. 27

We spent all day on the train. Arriving in Brest our ship was still in the dock. Therefore we had to sleep in the "Heldenkeller" [heroes' cellar, an air raid shelter].

Mon. Apr. 28

In the boatswain's mind, we needed a double work-out after so much rest. What we did in the morning wasn't exercise anymore, it was racing. Boatswain's mate Meetschen was the first one getting side pains from the racing around but he stayed with us to the end.

This was followed by artillery duty on the 10.5 cm with boatswain mate Albrecht. We gave part of the ship a new coat of paint, untangled the lines and made Zeisinge (short utility lines and fancywork that are used to tie together equipment or dress up the ship). And that was it for the day. In the evening we stayed on board because we had watch duty. While on post in the front of the ship, the air raid warning was given. The crew had to move to an air raid shelter. But nothing happened.

Tues. Apr. 29

After we cleaned the ship, I had to get ready to pick up the mail. Today seaman Mung was going to show me how to do it. Tomorrow I am supposed to do it by myself. It took the whole afternoon. I took mechanic mate Kaiser's watch to avoid going in the "heroes' cellar". Again we had air raid warnings.

Wed. Apr. 30

I finished my mail and got on my way. I returned about noon. No duty this afternoon since we cadets were alone on board. We took over the whole watch since the starboard watch had gone to Tréboul in the morning. The port watch returned in the evening. Tonight we were not disturbed by air raids.

Thur. May 1

When we arrived at the railway station this morning we learned that there were no trains today, therefore we got 4 hrs of city leave. When we returned to the station a car was waiting for us. Thus we arrived in Tréboul about noon. Our hotel was in a beautiful location. In the afternoon we went to a movie.

Fri. May 2

We were gently awakened this morning. We started the day first with sport followed by breakfast. Afterwards we peeled potatoes and then played a soccer match against the engine personnel and won 4:1. In the afternoon Dietz and I went out to catch some crabs, which the cook prepared for us. Then we went out to Roches Blanches and played ping pong. Regrettably we had to be back at hotel at 2300.

Sat. May 3

After our morning sport we had to peel potatoes again. The weather was beautiful. We spent the morning and afternoon at the beach and played ping pong. In the evening we returned to Roche Blanches.

Sun. May 4

Today is our last day here, therefore the sun showed its best face. The marching band from the GNEISENAU played in front of its hotel. In the afternoon we hiked to Roches Blanches. We left at 1600 and stayed until evening.

Mon. May 5

After cleaning our hotel rooms we got ready for departure. We went to the railway station and arrived in Quimper later in the day. There we had a five hour layover before we continued to Brest. We volunteered for watch in the evening. The Tommies did not disturb us.

Tues. May 6

This morning there were more of us participating in our morning exercise since the engineering cadets joined us on board. The ship left the dock afterwards. It was followed by Signal duty. We went on Battle Station watch in the afternoon. At 2000 we dropped anchor at the anchorage.

Wed .May 7

At 0800, we were ready to go to sea. After PE we had Signal duty. In the afternoon we had to clean our stuff and update the log books. I had Battle Station watch 1600 until 1800. When I was awakened for signal watch at 2340, the Tommies paid us a visit again. The search lights scanned the sky and in no time they had a Tommy in the beam. Unfortunately the planes were flying so high. But despite of this the heavy batteries fired relentlessly.

Thur. May 8

Today's wake-up call wasn't until 0730. At 0830, we are ready to go to sea. After our morning exercise we had "role duty" until 1130, followed by signal duty. We anchored at the anchorage at 1700, and the crew members departing for shore leave were shuttled with the launch to Brest. I took care of my mail.

Fri. May 9

Following our morning exercise we practiced Morse signals and winking over time. We entered the harbor at noon and docked pierside to take on provisions. We left again 1500 and escorted the MŐVE to Tréboul. This wasn't unknown territory for us. Entering the bay we could see the beautiful place we had been to: Roche Blanches. We could see our hotel too. Sadly I couldn't go ashore because I had starboard watch. The night was quiet.

Sat. May 10

We weighed anchor at 0800 and sailed towards Brest. We practiced "(mine) search" until afternoon in the outlaying anchorage. We cleaned the ship all morning long, scrubbing and painting. We dropped anchor at 1800 at the anchorage. The launch transferred the liberty detail ashore.

Sun. May 11

Today is a rest day. After cleaning the ship we had muster by Ltn. Merkle at 1100. At 1400 after lunch we went sailing in the cutter. The captain and the engineering cadets were with us on board. I had watch from 1400 until 1600. During that time some of our airplanes returned from a mission. Otherwise nothing happened.

Mon. May 12

Today is also a rest day. The obligatory morning sport was followed by Signal Duty: Morse signals over time and flag signaling. In the afternoon we had artillery duty on the 10.5 cm. After dismissal, the liberty detail was free to go ashore.

Tues. May 13

No PE today. In its place we had to clean the ship. We pulled the gangway in, cleared the lines and cleared the deck. The rumor was that we had to bring the Chief of the 3rd Safety Division to Tréboul. After tying up at the pier we had signal duty, but we were interrupted and had to line-up at the "Wicklung" for muster. Captain Schiller awarded several of us the EK (Iron Cross). I was amongst the lucky ones and I am very proud of it. After Captain Schiller left we got ready to leave. In the afternoon we had lessons in Navigation and Service Knowledge. Then we went on Battle Station watch. Today we were sailing until 2200 before we anchored. I immediately went to my bunk because I had watch again at 0400.

Wed. May 14

When I got off the watch at 0600, it was very foggy and we couldn't go to sea as planned at 0800. After our sport we had artillery duty. The fog lifted around noon and we were able to go out to sea. During my Battle Station watch the heavy Flak was shooting at very high flying aircraft, probably a reconnaissance plane. From 1400 until 1600, we had to update our log books and clean up our personal belongings.

Thur. May 15

After our traditional morning sport, which we have renamed "Navy Standard Hops" we had artillery duty on the 10.5 cm. We took turns in that exercise. First we practiced sea target shooting and Flak shooting. In the afternoon we had Navigation and Signal lessons. After we anchored I had signal watch.

Fri. May 16

First sport, then line-up on deck. We were already outside the harbor when suddenly the command was given: "Buoy over board," "Cadets in the port cutter." This was the first time that we were sitting in the rescue cutter. Usually we were in the marine cutter. Since the buoy was dropped on the starboard side, the starboard cutter was the first there. We had signal duty after the cutters were hoisted back on board and secured. In the afternoon we had a lesson on the basics of firing guidance. We were dismissed at 1600 and dropped anchor at 1800.

Sat. May 17

After breakfast I went on Battle Station watch. Sport was canceled. Together with the Engineering Cadets we had Duty Procedures lesson, followed by a Navigation class with Ltn. Wilke. We anchored in the anchorage at 1600. Cadet Friederich and I operated the launch. Returning from ashore the last time at 2320, I just could stay up since my watch began at midnight.

Sun. May 18

Everything went according to plan. Wake-up call at 0730. From 0900 to 1100: "clean ship". Then we had to change clothes. Cadets

Fritze, Greulich and I were supposed to dine in the officer mess today. The food was outstanding. Especially good was the wine we were served at the end. I went ashore at 1700 and went to see a movie. The launch returned, with the cutter in tow, to the ship at 2200.

Mon. May 19

Today we had the written exam for our inspection. No sport though. After "clean ship", we assembled with fountain pen in hand in the mess. The first test was Signaling followed by Artillery. After lunch, it was Navigation's turn. When we thought that we were finished for the day, boatswain's mate Meetschen came rushing in and hollered: " Line up immediately for artillery duty at the 3.7 cm." As was normal before every inspection we couldn't do anything right for him. In his eyes we were dumber than dumb. We then proceeded to the 2 cm. Nothing worked there. I was glad when it was all over. I went on signal watch at 1830. At 0200 next day, I was relieved.

Tues. May 20

Today was the inspection. At 0900, we lined up on deck to report to the Commandant. Then we moved to the signal deck for signal duty followed by PE where we performed our "Marine Hops". This was followed by artillery duty on the front U-boat and torpedo boat gun, then Flak "Anton" and last but not least at the starboard 3.7 cm. When we arrived at deck for "Seamanship" the knotting lines were already there. Schadding had already placed everything needed neatly on deck. After we finished our "Knots and Splices" demonstration we lined up for a final review. The Commandant and we too were of the opinion that we had learned a lot during our first half year on board. We had no special duties in the afternoon. We had a lesson of "Service Knowledge" with Ltn. Merkle followed by bringing our log books up to date. I went ashore in the launch at 1745 because I urgently needed a haircut. I bought a few books in the military bookstore and returned to the ship at 2300.

Wed. May 21

At 0800, we were ready to go to sea. After PE we were dispersed to the different guns. I was assigned to Flak A. Today's practice went better than the one during yesterday's inspection. I think once we practice with the gun chief it will improve. After the shooting exercise we took the gun apart and had a theoretical lesson on it. Then we practiced manning the guns during an alarm. I went on Battle Station watch until 1230.

After lunch we had to cleanup of our personal belongings and update the log books. I returned to Battle Station watch at 1630.

After dropping anchor in the anchorage, Ekki and I were put in charge of the launch. It was a bad trip since the boat's fireman and boatswain were slightly tipsy. Beside that the water was pretty choppy, getting me all wet before I had tied up the boat. At 2200, Funk, Bubi, Ekki and I picked up the liberty detail and we got wet once more. I was glad when the launch was secured again.

Thur. May 22

I was on watch from 0400 until 0600. A wet fog blanketed the water and I could barely see SPERRBRECHER 4. Once in a while it was raining too. When I was relieved at 0800, I secured my hammock and got ready for breakfast. During "clean ship" we were informed that PE was at 0900, but after we had changed clothes everything was canceled. Instead all sea cadets gathered in the mess for classes. Lt. Merkel explained to us the different kinds of gun turrets and their effects. After lunch we had to clean up our stuff. To my surprise I had to darn big holes in my socks.

After signal duty we were taught the use of the international signal book by the Staff Signal Chief. Ekke and I went ashore at 1700 and went to the movies. After that we had a sumptuous dinner and returned aboard.

Fri. May 23

Because it was windy and rainy, sport and similar jokes were canceled. I climbed the aft mast and freed the command flag. We had a headwind of 7-8 kts when we left the harbor. The swell was big too, making our ship heave up and down. I was on sea watch until 1000. Then I went to the living deck to gather my belongings, getting them ready for packing.

***

[This is the last daily log book entrance. He spends a few days with his parents in Essen and his sister in Winterbach where he meets for the first time his niece, Frauke, before proceeding to the Naval Academy in Mürwick.

In April 1942, he picks up the narrative again and recaps what had happened during the last year. Probably because of the traumatic experiences of the last few months and weeks, his handwriting changed dramatically.]

***

After a short vacation in Essen [his home town] I went to the Naval Academy. I had a good time but school remains school. I was relieved when I got new orders. To my horror it was to another school. This one was the very last on my wish list. I expected everything but not this. Therefore the two months I spent there, were real torture. I had absolutely no interest in the stuff we were learning. During class I tried to look as disinterested as possible. Out of stupidity I told everybody, that I had no interest in this communication stuff. I assume that this was noted in my service record. This was my second largest disappointment after the incident at the Naval Academy. I have the feeling that schools are always bringing bad luck to me. I was surprised that I passed the Officer Candidate Course. Afterwards I just disappeared without fanfare from this hospital place named Flensburg. My new orders weren't to my liking either: "Heavy" (ship) says it all. And worst of all, it had to be the battleship GNEISENAU. At least I returned to my old port, Brest. Maybe I will see my SPERRBRECHER 1 there. While I was at the Academy the commander [of SPERRBRECHER 1] received the Knight's Cross. It is hard to describe how happy I was when he sent me a picture [of the event].

Loaded with suitcases I arrived in Brest on board the train called "Wilhelm Hinrichs". After registering we were left to our own resources. Nobody cared about us. The next day we, with all our stuff, moved into our assigned quarters. We felt so helpless on this huge ship. After my first exploratory walks I always had trouble finding our room again. But after a while I found my way around. I was assigned to the 1st Division Battle Station in the front of the E-room. This was one of the impossibilities: the 1st Division was at Station A where I was supposed to work, while all the people in the E-room were in the 2nd Division and had different duties. One just has to accept these things. Slowly I got used to the life on a "Heavy". Only the lingering around in a shipyard got on my nerves. [The ship was still in the dry dock for repairs.]

One day, I didn't believe my eyes, SPERRBRECHER 1 was tied up at the pier. After "clear deck" I had nothing better to do than to rush over and I was greeted enthusiastically. My cadet officer had been promoted to Oberleutnant z.S. All the signal mates were still there. We had a nice evening. What I didn't like was that they all felt sorry for me being on a "Heavy", because I didn't like it there either.

In the meantime we three Officer Candidates [from the Academy] were reassigned. Pedro stayed in the front turret. Wilhelm moved to the airplane telephony and I moved to the signal department. Finally I got out of the suffocating E. room and out into the fresh air.

Work on our ship went on day and night [repair of bomb damage] when suddenly word came down that we were departing in the evening. Finally this was something that made my heart beat faster. We departed under the cover of darkness. Ahead of us sailed SPERRBRECHER 1. During the night we steamed for miles and miles just checking out the engines. Everything was working fine. At dawn we shot some salvos with the 28cm and 15cm guns. It was an elating feeling to stand on the signal bridge. Sometimes the front of the ship submerged under a rolling wave and the spray reached all the way up to us on the bridge. Going to sea on a "Heavy" is exhilarating. Sadly they don't go out to sea often enough. In the afternoon we were back in the dock and boredom continued. Every day, even at night, we had battle drill. We practiced battle formation

66

images with interference. Does that mean we will see action soon? All of us are anxiously waiting for what will be next. So far we haven't heard anything specific but rumors are flying everywhere.

On February 12, it was announced that we were going out for a night maneuver. Loading ammunition and refueling had already been done. Shortly before 2000, the command for departure was given. Was today the day? Everybody was anxious. The tugs came alongside to help with the maneuvering. But as bad luck happened so often, an air raid warning was given and we did not go out. Everybody was ordered to the battle stations. As usually the Tommy dropped his bombs, some uncomfortably close but then they fell further away also. Shortly before midnight the alarm was over. All clear for the maneuver! We went out. But where to? Nobody knew. Ahead of us was the SCHARNHORST behind us the PRINZ EUGEN. Again SPERRBRECHER 1 escorted us out.

Figure 50 Our battlegroup on war march

We went 30 miles west, and then turned north. Nobody knew where we were going. Suddenly we turned northeast. Then word came from the commandant "all men to battle stations". The convoy was attempting to break through the Channel to the German Bay. Finally we knew our destination. I spent the whole night on the Admiral's bridge and sent Morse messages. I am not going into details. They are sufficiently known through reports. The Tommy was on alert but didn't discover us until we had passed the Calais Narrow. He shot at us with coastal batteries but did not hit. Then he sent airplanes and they came in masses. Our fighters and guns were on guard and blasted them out of the sky. Enemy formations trying to attack us were dispersed. We managed to hit one destroyer. PRINZ EUGEN ⸱ sank it and set another one ablaze. After that the formation fled. SCHARNHORST and GNEISENAU were hit by E-mines. But damage was minimal. We fought off air attacks until late into the evening. Then all was quiet. It was bitterly cold. For the first time this year I saw snow and ice.

Figure 51 Steaming through the Channel

The following morning after some erratic maneuvering we entered the Brunsbüttel lock. We stayed there for a day before we passed through the Canal [connecting the North Sea with the Baltic Sea].

Passing the Colonial School in Rensburg, the girls from the school greeted us enthusiastically. As we passed by our band played snappy march music and the girls waved to the beat.

Figure 52 GNEISENAU

In the evening we arrived in Kiel and dropped anchor in the anchorage, because the ice affected our maneuverability. The next morning we went into the dock [to have the damage repaired]. We did our routine watch. Work on the ship progressed rapidly. The propellers were already exchanged when in the night of February 27-

28 we were hit by bad luck. A bomb hit the forward part of the ship. The magazines in turret A (Anton) exploded. Nobody escaped alive. My division had the most fatalities. Through quick actions we saved what could be saved. The damage was huge: 117 dead, 49 from my division alone. The damage was temporarily repaired and over Easter we went to Gotenhafen [Eastern Baltic Sea].

[Note: the ship never saw action again. It was decommissioned. In March 1945 it was sunk in Gotenhafen as a blockade ship.]

April 13, 1942 (Gotenhafen)

While we are here, I am waiting longingly for my new assignment. I am supposed to go to the U-boat command. Every day I am waiting for a telex but the dispatcher is probably still in sunny hibernation. They just don't understand that this waiting can drive people crazy. My division is supposed to go on leave tomorrow or the following day. But we haven't heard anything yet.

Helga [his girlfriend] wrote that she is in the hospital with measles. One less thing to look forward to for the leave we are supposed to get. The last time I saw her was in Kiel just shortly before the bomb attack. Friends from Essen invited me to dinner for tomorrow. I probably can't go because I am on day watch. Today is my last day with the 1st Division because from tomorrow on, that "club" will not exist anymore.

April 14, 1942 (Gotenhafen)

This morning, getting ready for my day watch, a sentry of the 5th division was already there. Then on the way to the OB.F.z.S [Oberfähnrich zur See, probably equal to Ensign] I met Rolf who had the good news that our new commands had arrived. When I got to my room, Horst called: "You are going to the 7th U-boat Flotilla in St. Nazaire". I have seldom been as happy as today. I packed my suitcases in the afternoon and signed out everywhere. At 1745 I met Miss Gronemeyer and we went to dinner together. Later we visited one of her co-workers, whose last name I have forgotten. But her first name was Inge and she lived in the Adolf Hitler Street 100. We celebrated my new assignment with dance music from a gramophone and the radio. Inge is a great girl, a bit naughty but very pretty. I returned aboard at midnight.

April 14, 16, 17, 1942 on the train to France.

I got up at 0600 and left for the railway station because I had to check in my luggage. Wilhelm and Rolf who were assigned to the 2nd U-boat flotilla were supposed to come a bit later. They arrived too late (for the morning train) and therefore we left (for Berlin) at 1300. Nothing happened on the way to Berlin. Searching for accommodations in the evening, we almost walked our feet off. Finally, at midnight we found accommodations in the Alexander Barracks. We continued our travel to Paris at 0635 the next morning. In Hannover I gave Hildegard's father a note to call my parents and to tell them that the train was coming through Essen. That worked beautifully. When the train pulled into Essen main station, Inge and "Piglet" (his sister and niece Frauke) were on the platform waving furiously. We didn't have much time to talk because the train stopped only for 5 minutes. We then took care of Hildegard who was still very distressed due to the hero's death of her brother. I felt really sorry for the girl. At midnight we began celebrating Wilhelm's birthday. Naturally, we had to celebrate this. We arrived in Paris at 1830 and we dropped Hildegard off. After doing some shopping, we continued our journey at 0825 the next day. Arriving in Nantes, I left my two battleship comrades and continued on to St. Nazaire on a local train. Arriving there, I learned that the 7nd flotilla was berthed in La Baule. Therefore I went straight on to there. In La Baule I reported to the Commanding Officer and the Adjutant. I was told to check into the Hotel Roseraie and to come back the next morning. That gave me time in the evening to explore the city. I can only say that it is beautiful here. All the houses are small, gabled houses hidden amongst pine trees. The big hotels adhere to the local building style. It is very obvious that this region of France caters to the very rich. This is just good enough for us.

April 28, 1942 La Baule

I reported to the Adjutant at 0900. Fortunately he kept it short: "Braun, you are reporting to U-593. Report to the Commandant and the 1st Watch Officer." My commandant was still asleep when I arrived at the Hotel Celtic. I left and returned again at 1000. I had been waiting for a short while when he came down for breakfast. After he finished I reported to him. He is a sharp-looking guy (Kptlt. Gerd Kelbling). After he explained my duties and other things I was dismissed and told to get my instructions from the 1st Watch Officer. I was sitting alone on the front of U-593 during lunch time. But I guess the others will arrive soon. In the afternoon I stowed my belongings away and brought the log book up to date.

***

[Here end Günter's actual diary entries. More than a year later, after his death at sea on U-436 (under the command of Günther Seibicke), Günter's personal belongings, including this log book, were returned to his parents, my grandparents. My grandfather, Fritz Braun, then continued the entries using letters and personal conversations with his son.]

Continuation of the log book by Fritz Braun

On April 20, 1942 U-593 departed to the American coast where it operated between New York and Philadelphia. After his return, Günter wrote the following letters to his parents. The letters are affixed in the log book.

On board June 18, 1942
Dear Parents
Today we were welcomed back (to home port) with music. To quell your worries I am writing you a few lines. During the last few months a lot of mail has accumulated here. But everybody has to wait a while for an answer because I have other things to do. Maybe we will get some leave now because we have to stay in port for a while (for repairs). There is a chance that I have to go to U.W.O (U-boat Watch Officer) school and then return here.

Now some details about our deployment. We spent the whole time between New York and Philadelphia sinking several freighters. But we "received" some depth charges also. One just has to live with these unpleasant things. All in all I like it here. We know at least why we deploy, we see obvious success. That makes even the days in the shipyard enjoyable. Today, our first day back here, I am on watch again. You get used to not going ashore. On the other hand I am glad (to stay on board) because I don't want to partake in the drinking binge tonight. Hopefully we will get leave and then I can tell you the rest.

How come mom keeps so silent? Had she already given up on me? I hope not.
I will end here
Greetings
Yours Günter
PS Don't write back. I am going to change command. Wait for my new address.

According to Günter's verbal report the boat, returning to St. Nazaire, was two weeks overdue having been tangled up with a convoy. While being pursued by a destroyer, the U-boat was severely damaged by a depth charge. They limped home on a southerly course and it was only through favorable weather that the boat was able to make it home on the last drops of fuel and the crew living only on coffee, lemons and cigarettes.

While the boat was in the dock for repair, Günter's education as a Naval Officer continued:

June 21-July 28 1942 Naval Academy Mürwick, 2nd Company

August 1, 1942 Promotion to Oberfaehnrich z.S.

August 1- Sep.21 1942 1st ULD (U-boat Learn Division) Pillau on PRÄTORIA (training vessel). This was to be his best school time.

September 27, 1942 End of course in Pillau. Destination orders to Berlin. There on September 28, 1942 Hitler addressed his young, to be promoted officers. Günter was amongst them.

October 1, 1942 return to Mürwick to Torpedo School. Participation in a course for UTO (U-boat and Torpedo boat guns on TS PATRIA.

November 1-21, 1942 Torpedo Launch Unit "Hugo Zeye" in Travemünde.

Then return to Mürwick to Marine Communication School for U-boat Watch Officers. 2nd time on MNS MÜRWICK. Course ends December 17, 1942.

[Unlike his comrades who went on furlough after the boat's return, Günter, to his great chagrin, had to return to the Naval Academy in Mürwick for a half-year Watch Officer course. How he thinks about school shows in the following two letters.]

Mürwick June, 27, 1942

With some detours I landed in Flensburg again. Since I have to complete all my courses now, I will not return to sea duty for the next half year. After Mürwick I am probably going to Gotenhafen or Pillau. But this will not be happening during the next four weeks. At the moment they are trying to turn us rugged submariners into sharp soldiers –not an easy task. During the next few days I will be sending you RM 50.00 (Reichmarks) which I still owe you. I don't know where my military pay got stuck again. I have to find out in the next few days. Right now I still have enough money because eight weeks on war cruise pays well. I am sorry, but I have to ask for a favor again. I urgently need a couple of stiff collars because my soft ones have had it. I can't go anywhere with those anymore. Beside those I need some books: navigation text books, nautical tables and a blue notebook (for tactical navigation). It would be best if you could send anything that deals with navigation. In addition, please send me my postal book [the German postal service is also in the banking business and he is asking for his deposit book] because as long as I am here I can deposit quite a bit.

No news here. I just wish the school stuff would end as quickly as possible.
Günter

Mürwick, July 4, 1942

Dear Parents,
Thanks a lot for your letter. You weren't the only ones that were surprised. I was too. We were two days in port when I had to get on a train again. Sadly this time we didn't come through Essen or we could have seen each other again. I arrived here already two weeks late. The classes had already begun. But I already caught up with the things I had missed. Now I am going full speed from one course to the other and in the end I will be back on a boat as W.O. (Watch Officer). You can imagine how I am waiting for that day. Getting used to all the school stuff again wasn't easy for me. Fortunately the others from the boats feel the same way.

The word "leave" is presently not mentioned. I seldom get ashore. At the moment we have naval officers from Rumania here. We have to demonstrate some things to them. But I hope that when I am transferred from here in Flensburg to another school, that I can see Helga for a few days.

Yesterday, the Tommies did something crazy. They arrived about noon, dropped their bombs in the surroundings and then 4 or 5 of them were shot down.

I will end here because I still have to iron my pants.

Günter

Naval Academy Muerwick 1942

Figure 53 Günter Braun: third front row, center

Dear Mom,

I would have been happy had the collars been starched, because right now I have only dirty cloths left and I have no opportunity to have my cloths pressed.

I regret that I didn't have a chance to have my picture taken with a beard (after returning from the U-boat mission). They took some pictures of us on board with me in them. I have to see if I can get some. I myself was surprised about my beard. When I don't have to return to school after the next tour, I will leave it in place. You would think an old man is visiting you.

Günter

His father continues:

On December 18, 1942 our son returned home for a 3 week vacation. How happy mom, Inge and little Frauke who are also visiting were, is hard to describe. It has become rare to have both my children here over Christmas. To our greatest joy, Inge's husband Ernst, Frauke's father, who is in the Army announced his coming between Christmas and New Years. Thus my greatest wish to have our whole family together during the Holidays becomes a reality, a rare occasion during war years. I don't know if a premonition came over me that I wanted all my loved ones around me once more. But maybe it was supposed to be that way. Our boy was happy to be home again. He had so much fun with his little niece, romping around with her all day long. The happiness for our "little one" was complete when his friend, Wolf Klein, whom he hadn't seen since both entered the military, arrived on leave also. The two of them had so much to talk about, that they constantly were together either here or at the Kleins' apartment. In mid December Wolf was promoted to Lieutenant in the Army, while Günter expected his promotion to Leutnant zur See by January 1, 1943.

Christmas Eve 1942

Inge and I lovingly had decorated the Christmas tree. We did it for little Frauke and our big boy. Our little "flea" (Frauke) had a hard time to wait for the bell to ring, which called us all into the decorated room. Frauke was excited about the lit tree and all the presents Father Christmas had brought. For the rest of us he had brought presents reflecting the war circumstances. In solemn joy we pressed each other's hands. With all the hardship around us real Christmas cheer did not come over us. The irreversible tragedy of our 6th Army in Stalingrad weighed heavy on us. Günter especially became very silent. Where were his thoughts? With Helga or his comrades at sea or was it premonition? Each of us probably asked the question what the next Christmas would look like. Who will be missing under the Christmas tree? This Christmas Eve, which we all had envisioned much happier, ended in somber and serious conversation with our guest, Dr. Pollmann and the typical air raid alarm. To avoid a heavy heart one should not look in times like this into the future and what is lurking in the dark. This only paralyzes our will and resistance and makes us despondent and anxious.

New Year's Eve 1942

Christmas is over. Ernst will be here until after New Year. Günter and Wolf are working feverishly for the New Year's Eve celebrations. Somehow our two warriors were able to get hold of two suitcases of wine. They quickly discussed with mom what kind of punch to make for the evening and already prepared it under Günter's skilled hand early in the afternoon. Mom, Inge and grandma are working in the kitchen and all the preparations are intensively watched over by Günter. Under Günter's direction New Year's Evening turned into a happy celebration. The young folks, Inge and Ernst, Günter and Kaninchen, Wolf and Miss Claess had gathered in the living room while we "oldies", Grandma Clara, Mr. and Mrs. Claess (from next door), Mrs. Klein and Mr. Pirels gathered in the dining room. The punch and the cold plate were delicious and Günter's mixing skills were greatly admired. At midnight Günter appeared in his white mess jacket and proclaimed: "The young ones wish the oldies a Happy New Year". We raised our glasses in a toast. I thanked in the name of the "oldies" and wished our three present soldiers all soldiers' luck for 1943. We retired after midnight while the young folk celebrated into the wee hours.

Sunday, the 3rd of January.

Günter received a telegram from Helga and she is expecting him. Our boy is happy. His train for Hamburg and his two day visit with Helga is leaving at 1209. On January 6, 1943 he has to report to a ship artillery course in Swinemünde. At 2200 an air raid alarm sounded. Busses and trams stopped operating. Therefore Günter had to walk to the railway station and left already at 2300. With a last kiss and handshake he left into the deep, dark night, never to return.

Christmas 1942

Figure 54 The author and her father

Figure 55 The author and her uncle Gűnter Braun Christmas 1942

Figure 56 "The tall man in the dark suit" Günter Braun and his niece Frauke

Figure 57 Günter Braun and his friend Helga. The back of the picture is inscribed with: "to Frauke so she knows what her uncle Günter looks like." January 1943

81

His next training stations were:

From January 6 until February 1, 1943 Ship artillery course in Swinemünde on the ship SAS GENERAL OSARIO.

On January 1, he was promoted to Ltn.z.Sea. The promotion document already awaited him in Swinemünde. Practice shooting during a storm and severe cold was not as successful as expected. He also got frost bites in both ears and wrote about this: "my ears are hanging down like the ones of a German shepherd dog and hurt a lot."

From February 1 until February 25, 1943 he is assigned to a Flak course on the vessel WANGONI which is moored next to the OSARIO. His opinion about the course: "Flak is a philosophy of life."

On February 25, 1943 Günter called home from Berlin to inform his parents that he was assigned to the 6th U-boat flotilla in St. Nazaire. He was in good spirits.

On March 1, 1943 he began his duty as 2nd Watch Officer on U-436. A few days later he was sent to an eight day course in Ostenende (Belgium). Through a comrade who was going on leave, he tried to find out if his parents in Essen had survived the bombing raids on the city on March 5 and 12, 1943. Through the same comrade his parents learned that their son himself survived a bombing raid just with his bare life and that all his belongings were burned. On March 28 he writes home that they were going out to sea soon and that their probable return was late June to early July 1943.

On board March 28, 1943

We are leaving soon. Our boat is ready again and I am ready to go.

Many thanks for your cards and letters. I am happy that you got the crate [he had sent food items home from France]. I was afraid the bottles of oil wouldn't survive the journey.

I also wrote to Kaninchen [a family friend]. The poor girl had to wait so long for mail. But I have had and had still have my hands full.

Next time I come home on leave I will bring some nice things again. It is so difficult to ship anything from here. When I get the pictures from Swinemünde and they turned out nicely I will send one to Helga and Mano as promised.

So, don't worry when you don't hear from me for a long time. Wish us good luck and that we are successful.

Greetings and Kisses
Günter.

This was his last letter. On May 26, 1943 U-436 under the command of Guenther Seibicke was sunk at 43-49N, 15-56W (North Atlantic off Cape Ortegal, Spain) by the British Frigates TEST and HYDERABAD. Boat and crew were a total loss.

LETTERS

I recently discovered a photo album from his high school years at the NPEA Oranienstein. In that album I found some letters I had no idea they existed.

The first is dated February 7, 1941, the day after he learned that he had become an uncle (I was actually born on January 29, 1941 but it took a week for him to get the news). The letter is addressed to his sister, my mother, who was two years his senior but about 1 foot shorter than he.

My dear, little sister

I think I was waiting as much here as you at home (for this baby). Whom does the little one resemble, the father or mother? I am sure she didn't get anything from her uncle. But then, when I was her age I was already more mature. It's probably a gender thing. Does she make a lot of "music"? There is nothing better than a strong voice. You become aware of that when you are standing here · on the bridge of the Christian Seafaring trying to get your wishes across to the other people. I myself wished for a boy. But when our "Fienchen" (nickname for the new baby) turns out like her mother I can take her on a pub crawl in the future, like you did with uncle Walter. I can't wait to see our little one. But here I am so far from home. But I think before we transfer to Mürwick I will drop in at home. But now uncle Günter has to trumpet to all his friends the good news, that I have gotten a little one.

Congratulations and best wishes to Frauke too

From your old seafarer

Günter

Greetings to Oma and Opa, Papa and the Grand- grandmothers. Please don't forget little Heini

A week later on Feb. 15, 1941 he writes again to his sister, the new mother:

Dear little, new mama
Thanks for your card signed by all the relatives. Looks like Daheim 3 (street address) has become a hostel. I am more and more amazed. Today I had a nice surprise: Mano (a family friend) sent me a little care parcel. I am overwhelmed that the faithful soul thought about me. I wrote her and complained that it was not nice of her to leave Essen now (she moved to Berlin). But I hope to see her in the near future.

The second surprise came from "Ltn. Senior" Rehfeld. He sent me a card inquiring about my whereabouts. I answered him too. Getting a surprise is always a nice change. I told him too about our family addition. I have to close now because I am running the launch today and have to pick-up the liberty detail from shore.

Greetings to all and for you a kiss
From your Günter
PS; I don't have envelopes anymore!!! SOS

A letter written to my uncle by my mother, his sister, dated May, 23, 1943 seems to be a premonition.

The letter was returned to my mother on July 8, 1943 with the stamped note:

Return! Recipient missing in action.

The letter reads:

Herchweiler, May 25, 1943

My dear "big" brother,
Today I am thinking a lot about you and therefore I will write you a few lines. Who knows when you will receive these, but when you return to shore you will be happy to find these greetings.

I finally said farewell to Legau (a small town in Bavaria, where had stayed for several months). On April 15 we got an apartment in Baltersweiler, one rail stop from St. Wendel. I am glad that we finally have our own household again and that "piglet" has space to roam. Right now we are still in Herchweiler and helping grandma because Line (her daughter) had to go to a sanatorium for three months. Tomorrow evening mom will arrive here. I don't know how long she will stay. Our little "flea" makes good progress and she knows the whole village already. One can either find her in the cow or the horse barn and she speaks the local dialect already well.

So, big brother, I hope you will soon be back from a successful war cruise.

Many greetings and hugs
 I remain
Your Inka and Frauke

After the news of Günter's death at sea reached his military prep school, his father, my grandfather, received the following letter:

June 6, 1944
National Political Education Academy Oranienstein, Headmaster of the School

Dear Mr. Braun
The announcement of your son's, our comrade's heroic death ended all hope, which we had tied to the news that he was missing. Together with you, Mr. Braun, your wife and your family, the NPEA Oranienstein mourns a good and brave comrade, who was held in high esteem for his modesty and diligence by his teachers and loved by his schoolmates. He was class president and later as Youngman marching band leader and in his responsible demeanor was great help in the living quaters of the school and as the Hundertschaft (an organized group of hundred students)leader. He had great influence on the younger students. The news of your son's heroic death will deeply move his comrades at the Front.

In the name of the faculty, the Youngmen (students) and all employees, I am sending my heartfelt condolences to you, your wife and your family for the irreplaceable loss you encountered through the heroic death of your son. Please also send our condolences to your son's fiancée. I wish her a brave heart despite the great pain she has encountered.

I hope your son's exemplary demeanor and the knowledge that many are mourning his death is some kind of consolation during the time of your sorrow.

Heil Hitler

Answer to the letter from June 6, 1944

June 21, 1944
To the headmaster of the NPEA Oranienstein

My sincere thanks, also in the name of my family, for the your letter from June 6, 1944 in which you expressed condolences at the heroic death of our beloved boy. It fills us with pride to hear from you in what high esteem he was held at your facility and to hear from his Flotilla Commander that Günter was in every way a hopeful officer who embodied in his demeanor and thinking a true Oranian Youngman spirit.

I feel obliged to thank you and all who had part in our son's education and for the great educational work during a time when Oranienstein was his second home.

I am convinced that after a victorious war when an Honor Roll of Oranienstein's Youngmen, who with their unfettered belief in our eternal Germany went to their early death, Ltn.z.S. Günter Braun, one of yours, who far from home in the Northeast Atlantic was killed in heroic action with the enemy and in fulfillment of his duty, will be fondly remembered.

With fondness for Oranianstein
Heil Hitler
Fritz Braun

THE SHIPS

SPERRBRECHER 1

Sperrbrecher 1

Built in 1935 as cargo ship SAAR

Requisitioned by German Navy on Sept. 17, 1939 and transformed into a minesweeper/ school vessel.

Armament: 2x10 mm guns, 2x37mm Flak guns, 15x 20mm machine guns.

Sunk on August 26, 1944 in the harbor of Brest during a RAF air raid.

Note: Sperrbrecher ships were larger cargo vessels armed and used by the German Navy as minesweepers. They led convoys through minefields and escorted U-boats out of harbors. In the forward cargo holds they contained large electrical generators, sometimes aircraft engines, to produce a big magnetic field to detect and explode mines. The bows were strengthened and often their cargo holds were filled with buoyant material for keeping them from sinking in case of hitting a mine.

Figure 58 Sperrbrecher 1

Sources:
http://www.wrecksite.eu/wreck.aspx?59392
http://www.german-
navy.de/kriegsmarine/ships/minehunter/sperrbrecher/index.html
http://en.wikipedia.org/wiki/Sperrbrecher

Crew of SPERRBRECHER 1 Jan.-May 1941

As compiled from the log book

Captain	Jakob
Ltn.	Wilke
Ltn.	Schmidt
Ltn.	Schönfelder
Boatswain mate	Traumitz
Boatswain mate	Ramen
Boatswain mate	Schmidt
Boatswain mate	Albrecht
Seaman	Fritze
Seaman	Henne
Boatswain mate	Meetschen
Chief machine mate	??
Deck Chief "Schmadding"	??
Helms mate	Baum

Seaman	Greulich
Shipmate "Smudje" (cook)	Pröpper
Boatswain's mate	Kamm
Fireman	??
Boatswain mate	Lüders
Boatswain mate	Doerz
Seaman	Mung
Mechanic mate	Kaiser
Plus about 20 naval cadets	

Battleship GNEISENAU

May 21, 1938 Commissioned
May 16, 1939 Becomes Flagship of the German Navy
May 1939 - March 1941 Together with battleship SCHARNHORST sinks 22 ships (14 by GNEISENAU)

March 22, 1941 Both ships homeported in Brest, France

April 6, 1941 GNEISENAU hit by aircraft torpedo and damaged, put into dry dock.

April 11, 1941 Hit by 4 bombs during an air raid on Brest. Over 100 fatalities.

Feb.11-13, 1942 Battleships SCHARNHORST, GNEISENAU and PRINZ EUGEN escorted by 6 destroyers (PAUL JAKOBI, RICHARD BEITZEN, FRIEDRICH IHN, HERMANN SCHOEMANN, Z25, and Z29) and 14 torpedo boats break through the English Channel, to return to Kiel, Germany. GNEISENAU is hit by a mine on the way to Kiel. Put into drydock in Kiel for repair.

Feb.26-27, 1942 Hit by a large bomb, exploding Turret A and the whole front Section of the ship. 146 casualties.

April 4, 1942 Moved to Gotenhafen (Gdynia), to be decommissioned.

Jul.1, 1942 Withdrawn from service

March 27-28, 1945 Sunk as blockade ship in Gotenhafen.

1947-1951 Broken up and scrapped.

Besides being damaged in war action, the GNEISENAU was damaged in an Atlantic storm in November 1939 and required repairs in Kiel. Again on Dec.28, 1940 she was damaged in a storm.

Figure 59 Gneisenau

Sources:
http://www.german-navy.de/kriegsmarine/ships/battleships/gneisenau/history.html
http://www.german-navy.de/kriegsmarine/ships/battleships/gneisenau/operatrions.html
Günter Braun, log book

U-593

Type: VII C
Launched Sep. 3, 1940
Commissioned Oct. 23, 1941

Commander: Kptlt. Gerd Kelbig (until sinking on Dec.13, 1943 in the Mediterranean; all 51 survived)

Figure 60 Gerd Kelbig official portrait and after a war patrol

U-593 had 16 war patrols. On the 2nd cruise leaving St .Nazaire, France on April 20, 1942 to patrol the US east coast between New York and Philadelphia, U-593 was damaged but limped home after being 21 days overdue.

Figure 61 U-593 sinking

Source: http://www.uboat.net/boats/patrols/u593.html
Log book Günter Braun

U-436

Type VII C
Launched June 21, 1941
Commissioned Sep. 27, 1941
Commander Kptlt. Günther Seibicke (commanded the boat until
May 26, 1943 when it was sunk with all hands lost)
8 war patrols

Figure 62 Günther Seibicke Official portrait and after a war patrol

Figure 63 U-436 sinking

Source: http://uboat.net/boats/patrols/u436.html

British Naval Archive records

May 26, 1943
15:27 BST

Position: Lat 43° 49' N
           Long 15° W

Ships involved: HYDERABAD, TEVIOT, TEST, TRENT, ERNE
and OXLIP

June 16, 1943

To Commander in Chief, Western Approaches
Report of proceedings of Convoys K.X. 10 and O.G. 90

A successful voyage in which no merchant vessels were lost. The only contact with the enemy resulted in the destruction of a U-boat by TEST and HYDERABAD. The hunt commenced with a smart and accurate counterattack by TEST, close to the convoy. A deliberate attack was later carried out by TEST, followed by a deliberate attack from HYDERABAD. Recorders from the latter ship have not yet been received. Wreckage of a definite U-boat character was recovered by both ships and samples from the TEST have been forwarded to the director of Anti-Submarine Warfare. In view of TEST's failure on 4th March, which resulted in a Board of Inquiry, this fine effort was particularly satisfactory, and their attention to training and resultant efficient drill, has quickly reaped reward.

G.W.G. Simpson

Commodore (D)

Excerpt of letter of proceedings of convoy KX10 OG90

H.M.S. TEVIOT
31st May, 1943

At 1415Z/26 in position 43 degrees 50 mins North 16 degrees West TEST obtained contact on starboard bow of convoy which he classified as submarine. I ordered TEST and HYDERABAD to hunt until convoy was clear, but to rejoin by dusk. After two hours had relapsed and TEST had made no report, although group standing orders require him to do so, I asked for information and TEST replied he was remaining until 1715 Z and then rejoining. Believing from this signal he had satisfied himself that contact was fish which I indeed thought it was, I concurred. However next day TEST informed me that HYDERABAD and himself had secured wreckage, oil and flesh after their attacks. Had I been so informed, I should have detailed escort to remain and made necessary report to shore authorities. Commanding Officer of TEST, Lt. Commander Collinson, R.N.R has been informed by me of my opinion of this omission on his part to comply with group orders.

I have the honor to be,

Sir,

Your obedient servant.

S. Leigh

Senior officer, 44th Escort Group

TEST's report on A/S attacks is attached together with recorder trace and track chart. In addition to items of evidence mentioned in TEST's report (and which TEST has retained) a small piece of flesh was reported to have been picked up. This is available on TEVIOT.

Owing to the shortness of time spent at Gibraltar HYDERABAD's report has not been received, but it is understood that HYDERABAD also picked up oil, wreckage and flesh.

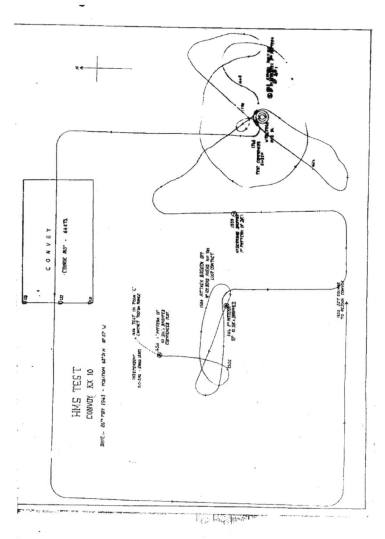

Figure 64 HMS TEST convoy KX 10

Afterword

Oct. 2, 2012

Happy Birthday Uncle Günter

You would turn 92 years today. Had the devastating war not snuffed out your young life so gruesomely would you be still alive? I know where your watery grave is. I know the names of the ships which hunted your ill-fated U-boat, U-436, finally destroying it but staying at the spot until debris and flesh rose to the surface. It's all documented in the British Naval Archives and I have all that documentation. You know, that had you stayed with your original U-boat, U-593, you would have survived the war. It must have been a horrific situation when you limped home from the US coast after being hit by depth charges and you weren't sure if you could make it back to your home port in St. Nazaire, France. People had given up on you, you were 21 days overdue. As you know, the boat was repaired and returned to sea again but was sunk in December 1943 in the Mediterranean Sea. Everybody survived. Instead, you were assigned to U-436 and this boat did not make it home.

In September 1944 SPERRBRECHER 1, the ship on which you got your sea legs, was sunk by RAF bombs in Brest harbor. I don't know if the crew survived the bombing. I had a chance to visit Brest several times during the last few years. My sister, who was born after the war, and her husband have a house nearby. I took a harbor cruise, saw the U-boat pens that are still there and visualized the buzzing activities in this harbor during the war. All the piers where the warships were tied up during your time are gone. In their place are now moored hundreds of fancy sailboats. The port cities of Brest, St. Nazaire and Lorient were destroyed on September 19, 1944. Allied bombers could not destroy the U-boat pens, so they destroyed the cities instead to keep supplies from flowing to the German ships.

I have only the blink-of-an-eye memory of you: I, just a month short of two years, ran towards a tall man in a dark suit. From your log book and some pictures I know it was Christmas 1942.

Now almost 70 years later, I got to know you, my uncle who greeted my arrival in this world with big fanfare. Yes, I know you were disappointed that I was not a boy. So, probably was my father because he treated me more like a boy in my formative years and instilled the love for technical stuff in me. His pet name for me was "Heinrich" (Henry). But I can assure you, I would have been thrilled to go on a pub crawl with you at the appropriate age. I actually did one with your uncle Adolf in London. You never had a chance to see the charm of British pubs. All you knew were the Brits, the "Tommies" as you called them, dropping bombs on you and sinking ships. In 1955, I visited England for the first time and returned several times in later years. I got to love that country. You know that uncle Adolf, aunty Leni and cousin Eric had moved to England when life in Germany became too dangerous for Adolf, who was Jewish. Actually Eric was born in England. They became my favorite relatives and drew me back to England frequently. Leni and Adolf are gone now but I still have contact with Eric, your cousin.

I have your ship log book now. It had been returned with your other belongings to your parents, my grandparents, after your boat did not return. From there it was handed down to my mother, your sister. Now I am in possession of it but will donate it to the Mariners Museum here which is interested in this historic document. I am in the process of translating it into English. It is ironic that the part of the US you patrolled with a U-boat became my home almost 30 years later. I moved here with my family in 1970 and we can boast of having the largest harbor in the world which is home to the 6th US fleet. All the nuclear-powered aircraft carriers are built here in Newport News, our town. You complained about the impersonal life on the GNEISENAU with its crew of 1600. Imagine life on a carrier with a crew of 5000. It's a floating city with a huge flight deck on top. About 150 ships call Hampton Roads home and I had a chance together with my son Dirk to spend a day on the Missile Cruiser VIRGINIA as guests of the captain and then later we cruised on the aircraft carrier INDEPENDENCE as guests of one of the pilots. But

I have never gotten a chance to go on a U-boat and put myself in your shoes, although I have been on a WWII boat that is on exhibition in Kiel now. I have been wondering how you, as tall as you were, fit into that confined space. During that visit in Kiel I also went to the U-boat Memorial and I saw your name etched in granite. You know, in Washington we have a similar memorial honoring the fallen of the Vietnam War. I get the chills every time I go there and see name, after name, after name. It is all so senseless.

You inquired once through a friend who was passing through Essen, if we had survived certain bombing raids on Essen. Yes, we all survived these and the war. The house was damaged. Incendiary bombs burned holes through the ceilings of two stories, but your father who always stayed in the house during the bombings, threw them out with a shovel thus saving the house. There were times when we had no windows, no electricity, no gas or water and we often spent days at a time in air raid shelters. Remember that concrete "cube", the two story bomb shelter near the Nightingale Valley? It survived the war after sheltering many people during the bombing raids and housed a furniture factory after the war. Finally they tore this eyesore down. I went there frequently, just standing in front of it and thinking back to those turbulent times. We did not spend the last months of the war in Essen. Your father had been drafted back into the Army again at age 51 to defend the Fatherland. My father, your brother-in-law, was at the Russian front, nobody knew where. Mom and I made our way to Bavaria where your mother already had gone. That's where we were when the war ended. Germany lost the war; the 1000-year Reich and Hitler did not survive. Hitler, the coward, took his own life. Many cities were totally destroyed. The country was divided amongst the Allies and later between the Soviet Union and the West with country under Soviet rule on one side, the East and the western allies in the West. We, in the Saarland became part of France. As Churchill put it "from Stettin in the Baltic to Trieste in the Adriatic an iron curtain has descended across the continent." (Churchill's speech at Westminster College in Fulton, Missouri, on March 5 1946). Millions of people were killed and displaced. Our family was one of the few lucky ones.

After the war, two years after your death, mom and I found our way back home to the Saarland and our apartment there. Dad came back in September 1945. I was one of the few in school who still had a father after the war. Some hard years followed, years of food shortages and reconstruction. Dad never could get rid of his war memories and suffered from nightmares until he died at age 91. He never talked about his experiences. I am wondering how you would have coped with all your memories: the mines that went off uncomfortably close to your first ship, the night raid on the docks in Brest where you and your buddies' quick action prevented a fuel train from blowing up, the devastating bombing of the GNEISENAU, the almost- demise of U-593? By the way, the captain of U-593 lived until 2005. Too bad I just found out about it recently or I would have contacted him to learn more about you and that harrowing war cruise that almost became your first and last one. These days we have a thing called "Internet" and it's there that I found out so much about your Navy time and what had happened afterwards. In 1991, I accompanied two naval historians to Germany to interview three still living U-boat captains from "Operation Drumbeat", the first group of five U-boats that came to the US coast just before you did. The Admiral in charge of this stretch of coast, Admiral King, didn't believe the Brits that German U-boats were on the way to the US coast. He thought that they did not have the reach. He learned the hard way that they had. On that trip I got a chance to visit the Mürwick Naval Academy, an imposing building. I have your 1942 class graduation picture that was taken in front of the Academy. One of the captains we interviewed must have been your torpedo instructor at the Naval Academy: Reinhard Hardegen of U-123 fame.

Your father spent two years in an Internment Camp in Bavaria awaiting his "denazification" (whatever that is). I still have letters he wrote to me from there. I could read and write before I started school. Thus all his letters are written in capital letter print and lavishly and lovingly illustrated. He came back in 1947 and died a broken man two years later from Multiple Sclerosis. But he still got to see his second grandchild, my sister Heike, who was born in 1946. I am wondering if you would have raised so much fuss about her as you did when I was born.

Your parents returned to Essen after the war but had to live in one room in a strangers' apartment, having to share a kitchen and bathroom. Essen was devastated, 97% gone, a wasteland of rubble. Your father returned to his old workplace until MS made working impossible for him. Most the old family friends in Essen survived and I got to know almost all of them. Wolf Klein who celebrated that last New Year's Eve (1942) with you returned from the war and became my surrogate uncle, so much so that when I started flying gliders he supported my hobby financially with the comment "Your uncle would have loved it". He founded a detective agency.

I saw in the photo album I have from the time you were at the NPEA Oranienstein that you got a chance to soar too at the famous Wasserkuppe, in a SG38, a flying broomstick. You should see today's gliders: slick, technically advanced fiberglass flying machines with reaches that were unimaginable in your time, reaches of thousands of kilometers.

I studied chemistry and after college returned to Essen in 1962 to work at the Essen-Mülheim airport at an aeronautical research facility. It was there that I got into soaring. It was also there that I met my future husband. We married two days after my birthday in 1969. He too became a glider pilot. Our son Dirk was born in Mülheim in September of that year. He too became a glider pilot. Exactly two weeks before his birth your mother died of cancer. She was only 69 years old. I had lived with her for 7 years. Something unimaginable to you happened that year: the first human set foot on the moon. Can you believe that? We all could watch it on TV, an invention that came after the war. Neil Armstrong, that first man on the moon, died just a few weeks ago.

What would you have become had you returned from the war? A farmer, as you had dreamed of as a young boy? I know you weren't scholarly minded, you hated school, any school. So I doubt if you would have returned to any kind of academia. But your teachers in Oranienstein and your superiors in the Navy lauded you, after your death, for your leadership skills. Maybe you would have become a politician. Or did you hate these too?

102

Oh, there are so many questions I would like to ask. But there is one more thing I have to tell you. Your sister's last wish was to be buried at sea. She wanted to be close to her brother. We honored her wish when she died in 1999. Her remains were dispersed off the coast of Wilhelmshaven on a cold, blustery January day in a beautifully conducted, dignified ceremony on board of a small ship. I never knew how close you two were until just recently when I found the letters you wrote to her after my birth.

Now, so many years later I have the feeling I finally got to know you, my uncle, through your log book. 70 years after your death I feel very close to you.

Happy Birthday again

Your niece Frauke

PS: In 1967, I was visiting your aunty Else and her two daughters, Ursula and Hilde, in San Diego, California. One day the German cruiser DEUTSCHLAND came into port to later join other ships for maneuvers. They had "Open House" and I got to visit the ship. While talking to one of the older crew members I told him that you were on the GNEISENAU in 1942. He asked for your name. When I told him he exclaimed: "What, the tall Günter?" I was stunned.

Figure 65 Gűnter Braun, March 1941

Acknowledgement

A big thank you to my ex-US Navy soaring buddies, who helped me with naval terminology and gave me a glimpse into the life on a war ship and a submarine: John Good, Robert "Boom" Powell, Al Fullerton and my Life Long Learning classmate Bill Peiffer.

Special thanks to Reiner Knudsen who was able to get the British reports from the Britisch Naval Archives.

Thanks to the curators of the Mariners Museum Library who encouraged me to translate the journal and who provided numerous helpful books; Mike Hostage, General US Air Force, who made the most useful connection for me to the German Navy in person of Lars Vergien,CDR(Jg)DEU Navy; to Uwe Paul, whom I met via the Internet and who provided many explanations. Thank you very much to Erica St.Dennis and Alisandra Snyder for their proof reading and corrections. A special thank you to Nick Thomas for his formatting work. Without his help the project would never have been finished.

Last not least, I am grateful to my late uncle Ltn, z.S.Guenter Braun, who kept the journal as part of his naval education and to my grandfather who completed the story up to the sinking of U-436.

About the Author

Frauke Elber, nee Jung was born on January 29, 1941 in Essen, Germany. In 1970 she moved with her family to Newport News, Virginia where the movie "A Bridge too Far" awoke her curiosity about events she remembered from World War Two. In 1999, after the death of her mother, she came in possession of her uncle's ship journal. In 2012 she decided to donate this journal to the Mariners Museum in Newport News and consequently decided to translate the German text into English. She is married to Wolf Elber, PhD and they have one son (who studied history)

Figure 66 German U-boat Memorial Möltenort/ Germany

Photo: Karl-Josef Schmeink

Figure 67 German U-boat Memorial Möltenort/ Germany Photos Heinz Potrafki

107

Made in the USA
Charleston, SC
20 October 2015